GOD'S TIMETABLE
FOR THE 1980's

Dr. David Webber
Radio Pastor
Southwest Radio Church

Copyright © 1984 by David Webber
Printed in the United States of America
ISBN 0-910311-14-5

— FOREWORD —

In this book of prophecy and current events we have endeavored to deal realistically with the end-time scenario as revealed in God's holy Word. The converging events of the ages compel us to look to the Bible for a picture of the last days of man's dispensation.

In detailing *God's Timetable* for this decade we have emphasized and analyzed a wide spectrum of subjects including the weather, outer space, robots, computers and the new age movement. My conviction is that this concise volume will help many people to better understand the developments in our fast-changing world and to have a sharper perspective of world events in the light of Bible prophecy.

Startling events are happening every day in the expanding world of communications. For example, N.E.C. Cellular Systems from Japan offers the fastest phone on wheels utilizing 666 possible channels. This mysterious number 666 (see Revelation 13:18) is occurring more and more in communications, banking and business. The number 666 will one day polarize the computer code marks and identification numbering systems of the Antichrist.

May God bless and use the written Word to reach the exploding masses of earth's population with the more sure word of prophecy and to see and believe on Him who is the central figure of all prophecy (Revelation 19:10).

David Webber

APPRECIATION

The author wishes to express appreciation to the Rev. Noah Hutchings of the Southwest Radio Church for his research which was invaluable in the preparation of *God's Timetable for the 1980's*. Rev. Hutchings is editor of *The Gospel Truth*, a publication of the ministry of Southwest Radio Church and is read and reproduced in the United States and in several foreign countries.

CONTENTS

CONTENTS

1

WHAT ABOUT 1984?

Ever since Eric Blair — whose pen name was George Orwell — wrote the novel *1984* in 1948, many people have looked forward with a mixture of excitement and trepidation to this cryptic and Orwellian date of 1984.

Walter Cronkite in his preface to George Orwell's *1984* wrote, "'Big Brother' has become a common term for ubiquitous or overreaching authority, and 'newspeak' is a word we apply to dehumanizing babble of bureaucracies and computer programs."

It is debatable whether we will see the dark drab, monotonous world described by George Orwell materialize before our eyes. However, as you will discover in this direct and documented book on prophecy, the potential developments in all kinds of technology, especially electronics, already astound the peoples of the world.

One of the ominous things we will enlarge on in this volume is the projected National Identity Card for every American by 1984. We will also examine the greatly expanded services of Swift II, including voice transmissions and image transmissions for 1984.

It also seems that 1984 could be a decisive year for Israel — already the nuclear time bomb of the Middle East.

As we consider the 1984 numerical interpretation of the Hebrew calendar 5744, which spells out destruction, we wonder what will be forthcoming in 1984!

Walter Cronkite further states in his preface, "George Orwell was no prophet, . . . If not prophecy, what was *1984*? It was, as many have noticed, a warning: a warning about the future of human freedom in a world where political organization and technology can manufacture power in dimensions that would have stunned the imaginations of earlier ages . . . *1984* is an anguished lament and a warning that we may not be strong enough, nor wise enough, nor moral enough to cope with the kind of power we have learned to amass. That warning vibrates powerfully when we allow ourselves to sit still and think carefully about orbiting satellites that can read the license plates in a parking lot and computers that can tap into thousands of telephone calls and telex transmissions at once and other computers that can do our banking and purchasing, can watch the house and tell a monitoring station what television program we are watching and how many people there are in the room."

There are people around today who believe that Big Brother is already with us and that the regimentation of the human masses has already begun.

The *Seattle Post Intelligencer,* October 8, 1983, ran an article entitled "Artist's Posters Argue That We've Yielded Freedom To Big Brother," said:

"*1984* is already here, says the man whose stark, black and white posters of Big Brother have been staring from Seattle streets. Ron Porter, a lanky, 30-year-old artist, said he created the poster to let people know that the mindless, conformist totalitarian world portrayed in George Orwell's novel is with us now. Big Brother is the all-knowing, all-powerful ruler invented by Orwell. Porter's poster depicts an ominous, glowering character who vaguely looks like Clark Gable, Omar Sharif or a young Howard Hughes. Beneath the portrait is the warning: 'Big Brother is Watching You.'

"During the past few weeks, scores of the posters have been plastered on bridges, under-passes, buildings and freeway abutments. The artist, who pays his bills by working as a counselor to the handicapped, said people don't realize *1984* is already here because today's world doesn't fit all of Orwell's gloomy description.

" 'Orwell's world is stark, oppressive, gray and drab,' Porter said. Obviously, we don't have that. The U.S. is flashy, glittery and spectacular. But there's an emptiness, a lack to the texture of life. There's an atmosphere of oppression, untruth and manipulation.

"Porter said he first read *1984* when he was 15. He read the book twice a year after that and, lately, has been rereading it once a month.

"He finds new examples of Orwell's foresight all the time.

"Take the case of New York police setting up roadblocks for drunken-driving checks, Porter said.

"It gets drunks off the road, but it also monitors who and where people are going and creates a heavy presence.

"In Orwell's novel, three super powers regularly shift alliance so that the one on the outs gets savaged by the other two. That is what has happened to the United States, Porter noted. The Soviets, our allies in World War II, have become our enemies and the Chinese, our former enemies, have become our friends. What's alarming, the artist said, is that people accept these changes without question.

"The people are just like in the book, said Gary Trott, an unemployed steel fabricator who serves as Porter's production engineer. They don't have the determination, will or desire to change anything. They think everything is going along wonderfully.

"Porter said he drew his version of Big Brother by scrupulously following the description in Orwell's book."

It is a certainty that the world will one day be ruled by an absolute dictator.

We read about this in Revelation 13:7, 8, 16, 17: "... power was given him over all kindred, and tongues, and nations, and all that dwell upon the earth shall worship him, whose names are not written in the book of life of the Lamb ... and he causeth all both small and great, rich and poor, free and bond, to receive a mark in their right hand, or in their foreheads: and that no man might buy or sell, save he that had the mark, or the name of the beast, or the number of his name."

Although we were told in 1934 that the social security numbers would never be used for any purpose other than the system today, your social security number is on your driver's license, job applications and virtually any business trans-action requires evidence of your social security number. If the proposed nine-digit zip code is implemented by the post office in 1984, every citizen of the United States will automatically have a string of 18 digits (or three sixes) that identify him all over the world.

Add to this the proliferating universal product code and the endless numbering systems of so-phisticated computers and you have an expand-ing world of exponential curves and identifying numbers. It seems that man and his number will soon be wedded.

Of course people are already using all kinds of numbers in banking and business. So, many would doubtless welcome a single identifying row of digits.

A quote from the *Times Union,* Rochester, New York, October 25, 1982, comically explains what is happening to our generation:

The headline reads: "All-Purpose Number Would Simplify Life."

"The government is toying with the idea of giving us all numbers. If the legislation passes, we'll all have to carry national identity cards.

"Maybe one day we'll have the Universal Product Code imprinted on our palms, like a can of beans, so they can run us through a scanner hooked up to a computer. Then when we're stopped on I-49 for doing 56 mph the cop can wave his laser wand over our hand and discover that we're wanted for harboring an overdue library book, or that we failed to contribute to the Police Benevolent Fund.

"That's the dark side. Our liberty is endangered. But is there a bright side? There could be.

"A lawyer friend, whom I regard as a zealous civil libertarian, put it this way: 'Who cares?' he said, 'If they'd take away all my other numbers and just give me one, I think I'd be happier than I am now.'

"All of us are already staggering under a load of digits that would give an abacus a hernia.

"Every year a snoopy computer asks my Social Security number intimate questions about where I got my money and what I did with it. And every day a lot of strangers, probably armed with some kind of number, bombard me with junk mail in an effort to get what's left.

"No, I think the lawyer friend could be right. The days when a person could drop out of sight are just about over, anyway. There is not true liberty anymore, so what's the difference? Just give me a nice number that's easy to remember and works on my telephone as well as my water bill, ends in the digits of my wife's birthday and my shirt size and opens my bicycle lock, and I'll go quietly." — *Dick Dougherty.*

Another headline from a recent edition of *The San Francisco Chronicle* demonstrates how fast the computer link and numbering identification system is coming.

The headline says: "Calif. Banks Plan Pos/ Debit-Card Net by Late '84."

"By late 1984, California consumers will be able to purchase retail merchandise at point-of-sale (POS) with debit cards, now that five major California banks are putting a co-owned, shared POS network into operation.

"Projecting that date for market-test implementation, the banks have completed a feasibility study and agreed to move into the developmental phase with the project, according to Steve Yotter, vice president of electronic product development, retail marketing division, of the Bank of America. The banks plan to form a nonprofit corporation with the same name as the network, the InterLink Network.

"The proprietors will include Bank of America, Crocker Bank, First Interstate Bank, Security Pacific Bank and Wells Fargo.

"Yotter indicated that the InterLink Network is concentrating on three retail industries: general merchandising, supermarkets and discount stores and the oil industry. He said three retailer meetings have been held with positive reactions, although there are certain issues still to be considered during the developmental process.

"The technology needed at point-of-sale to conduct the transfer of funds electronically has not existed until now, he explained. There has been recent movement toward the installation of sophisticated point-of-sale equipment in order to allow for efficient handling of transactions. For instance, supermarkets are acquiring sophisticated scanning equipment and, in the oil industry, retailers are moving toward acquiring equipment that allows them to transmit electronically.

"The technology just hasn't be an there until about two years ago, Yotter continued, and now we can move ahead with point-of-sale. For the retailers, there is also the matter of peripheral equipment to add to their existing equipment, like the magnetic strip reader and the pen pad, and the other issues I mentioned.

"Over the long term, I see InterLink displacing checks, bank cards and, eventually, cash, he continued. We are moving towards an electronic environment. From the customer point of view, once he can use the system, he will find it a more efficient way to do business.

"According to Yotter, the oil industry has expressed particular interest in the debit card as payment alternative. He attributed this to the fact that, in the oil industry, checks or credit cards are sometimes no longer accepted. When customers must pay cash, he noted that they usually tend to buy five or ten dollars worth of gasoline whereas, if they could use a debit card, they might choose to fill up the tank because of the availability of funds through InterLink.

"The greatest advantage is convenience, Yotter said. The time it takes to write a check and go through that approval process, or the time it takes to use a bank card and for the clerk to get an authorization is lengthy, as well as requiring extra identification for either process. With InterLink the customer only needs his debit card and his personal identification number.

"There will also be more security for the customer, he added. No more loss of checks or bank cards. If the customer loses his debit card, the card cannot be used without his personal I.D. number, so it's safer.

"The way InterLink will work, Yotter explained, is that a customer will go into a retail location, which is identified with the InterLink logo. The customer takes his purchases to the checkout line and presents his debit card. The card is swiped through a magnetic strip reader, the customer enters his personal identification number on the pen pad, and the clerk enters the transaction, which is then routed through the communications network. After verification of the retailer and of the user's fund availability, the customer is issued a receipt.

"Yotter said the banks are hoping that the time elapsed from the clerk hitting the enter key to the issuing of the receipt will be 10 seconds."

We can readily see that this new cashless society system will be popular, fast and safe. It is expected to be in operation in a limited number of states by late 1984!

Electronic financial services in the home will achieve mass-market status by Christmas, 1985 — two years sooner than predicted last winter.

Quoting *U.S.A. Today,* September 8, 1983, an

article entitled "Home Banking Nearer:"

"Yankee Group projects that in two years, 4.5-million households will have computerized phones with built-in display screens.

"Home banking is not a gimmick or a loss leader; bank-at-home will be a profitable service ... by cross selling a wide variety of financial products through the same electronic pipeline," the article concluded.

Among the probable early leaders: Shearson/American Express, J.C. Penney Co., Inc., and Sears, Roebuck and Co.

There will possibly be a new international Credit-Debit Card as a transition step between cash and checks and strictly electronic banking. Visa gets our vote as the one card to replace all other credit cards. In the name Visa you already have the numerical formula given in Revelation 13:18, "Here is wisdom. Let him that hath understanding count the number of the beast: for it is the number of a man; and his number is Six hundred threescore and six."

VI in Roman numerals equals 6. S is the Greek letter sigma that equals 6. And the letter A in the Chaldean language (Babylon) stands for 6.

Visa already has big plans for the future as stated in a recent article in *U.S.A. Today*, October 17, 1983, entitled, "Visa Tests Credit Card of Future:"

"Some 50,000 Ohioans today begin using a prototype of the 'charge card of the future.' The Electron card, the key to Visa International's plan for a worldwide all-electronic payments system, is being introduced through four Banc One Corp. banks in the Ohio towns of Middletown, Milford, Sidney and Wapakoneta. Initially the card will be used only in automated teller machines, replacing the ATM card customers now use. Later this year Banc One customers also will use the card instead of cash or checks in local retail stores.

"Ultimately, their checking or savings accounts will be debited electronically — eliminating paper transactions. Visa's plan is that banks worldwide eventually will replace their ATM cards or regular Visa credit cards with the 'all-in-one' Electron card."

Will the growing problems of government, and mankind in general, cause the majority to surrender personal liberty to a world authority for the sake of survival? Certainly, such a decision would not be new.

Israel had a perfect democracy, in form that is, until problems relating to their form of government became so burdensome that they asked for a dictator. Almost all democracies and republics of the past have ended up as monarchies or dictatorships because succeeding generations are inclined to forget the values of liberty which prompted the institution of a government for the people in the first place. And, according to the Bible, at the end of the present age the problems of the masses will become so great that they will seek a saviour to find solutions.

Some of these problems that the nations would have to contend with, as prophesied in the Bible, are: lawlessness, weapons of mass destruction, world inflation, overpopulation and famine. We are informed that a bloc of ten powerful nations will meet and appoint a world ruler to initiate world money control, world food control and control of all economics, politics and religion.

We read in Revelation 17:13, "These have one mind, and shall give their power and strength unto the beast."

Seasoned political observers have feared for some time that the problems of this present generation, which rival those of the antediluvians, would become so great that the masses would opt to surrender all rights and property to a world dictatorship.

George Orwell prophesied that life by 1984 would become a mixture of horror and dreariness, where would be neither liberty nor privacy.

Orwell predicted that food, clothing and housing would be standardized where everyone except the ruling elite would be numbered, controlled and subsidized by the state. It is a sobering thought that the predictions of men of the past 30 years are now dove-tailing with the prophecies of Daniel, written over 2,500 years ago, and the prophecies of Jesus Christ and the Apostle John written nearly 2,000 years ago.

At the end of the age an order will go out that every man, woman and child in the world should be numbered. There will be seven years of war, famine and pestilence, such as the world has never seen.

But Jesus said, "And when these things begin to come to pass, then look up and lift up your heads: for your redemption draweth nigh" (Luke 21:28).

For those who do not know Jesus Christ as Lord and Saviour, there will be judgment instead of redemption. God's invitation to receive Jesus Christ is still open, if you will come to Him in faith believing (Ephesians 2:8,9).

2

THE
NEW AGE MOVEMENT
DANGER
REAL OR IMAGINED?

The greatest effort the world has ever witnessed in the producing of a universal leader acceptable to all religions and political factions is now in progress. Certainly, these many messiahs that are being heralded by the underground occult network are in themselves a sign of the latter years.

Jesus said of His Second Coming in Matthew 24:21-27:

"For then shall be great tribulation, such as was not since the beginning of the world to this time, no, nor ever shall be. And except those days should be shortened, there should no flesh be saved: but for the elect's sake those days shall be shortened. Then if any man shall say unto you, Lo, here is Christ, or there; believe it not. For there

shall arise false Christs, and false prophets, and shall show great signs and wonders; insomuch that, if it were possible, they shall deceive the very elect. Behold, I have told you before. Wherefore if they shall say unto you, Behold, he is in the desert, go not forth: behold, he is in the secret chambers; believe it not. For as the lightning cometh out of the east, and shineth even unto the west; so shall also the coming of the Son of man be."

Because the world will be in great danger of an impending catastrophe, this state of fear will provide fertile ground for many false messiahs to rise up with a multitude of plans to save the human race from extermination. The New Age Movement to this date has been the most pronounced progenitor of such pseudochrists.

The satanic attempt to produce a false christ, or as the Scriptures identify him, the Antichrist, is as old as the original sin in the Garden of Eden. It has appeared in many forms and under many labels in the history of mankind.

When Satan tempted Jesus Christ to fall down and worship him, the Devil was actually offering Jesus an opportunity to follow him in rebellion against God and become the Antichrist.

God divided the nations and any attempt to unify the world under one single man before Christ comes to be King of Kings is of Satan.

The League of Nations, and later the United Nations, both failed to unify mankind under one form of government and one governmental leader because they offered only political solutions.

The New Age Movement recognizes that man is also a social and spiritual being, therefore, it incorporated into it social and religious panaceas to the turbulent human masses.

Constance Cumbey in her book *The Hidden Dangers Of The Rainbow,* provides the following definition: "According to the New Age sources, the New Age Movement is a worldwide network. It consists of tens of thousands of cooperating organizations. Their primary goal, or the secret behind their 'unity-in-diversity,' is the formation of a 'New World Order.' The Movement usually operates on the basis of a well-formulated body of underlying esoteric or occult teachings ... The New Age Movement, called by Marilyn Ferguson 'The Aquarian Conspiracy,' and deriving its name from the so-called Age of Aquarius, encompasses a number of groups and submovements, such as: The Holistic Movement, Humanistic Psychology, Transpersonal Psychology, Humanistic Movement, New Thought, Third Wave, Third Force, The New Spirituality, the Human Potential Movement, Secular Humanism and Humanism."

Evidently the New Age Movement thought that the year 1982 was the right time to bring forth its own christ, and the Christian world was startled when on April 25, 1982, full-page ads appeared in major newspapers in the United States and other nations. These messianic, paid ads stated in part: "In Answer To Our Call For Help, As World Teacher For All Humanity, THE CHRIST IS NOW HERE ... Since July 1977, the Christ has been emerging as spokesman for a group or community in a well-known modern community ... Throughout history, humanity's evolution has been guided by a group of enlightened men, the Masters of Wisdom. They have remained largely in the remote desert and mountain places of earth ... At the center of this 'Spiritual Hierarchy' stands the world teacher, Lord Maitreya, known by Christians as the Christ ... He has not as yet declared His true status, and His location is known only to a few of his disciples ... the Christ will acknowledge His identity and within the next two months will speak to humanity through a worldwide television and radio broadcast. His message will be heard inwardly, telepathically, by all peoples in their own language. From that time, with his help, we will build a new world ..."

The "christ" turned out to be a Hindu guru from Pakistan residing in London. The ads were sponsored by an organization for the New Age Movement, Tara Center, with main offices in London, New York and North Hollywood. The promoter of Lord Maitreya as the "christ" was Benjamin Creme, a wealthy Englishman.

Tara, a Hindu goddess, gave birth to an illegitimate son, according to the Hindu religion, 2,500 years ago. His name was Maitreya. Maitreya had supposedly been waiting for over two millenia for his revealing to humanity as the messiah. When the press failed to give Maitreya even token exposure, the only cost in Creme's Pentecost was the enormous sum it took to pay for the ads.

A few months later Lucis Trust added its voice and money to help Tara bring forth the "christ" by sponsoring a full-page color ad in *Reader's Digest*.

The October 1982 edition of this widely read publication carried their "lord's prayer," THE

GREAT INVOCATION:

> *From the point of Light within the Mind of*
> *God*
> *Let Light stream forth into the minds of men.*
> *Let Light descend on Earth.*
> *From the point of Love within the Heart of*
> *God*
> *Let love stream forth into the hearts of men,*
> *May Christ return to Earth.*
> *From the center where the Will of God is*
> *known*
> *Let purpose guide the little wills of men —*
> *From the center which we call the race of*
> *men*
> *Let the Plan of Love and Light work out*
> *And may it seal the door where evil dwells.*
> *Let Light and Love and Power restore the*
> *Plan on Earth.*

"The Plan" of the New Age Movement that all men are supposed to pray for is simply Satan's plan to enthrone his own king, the Antichrist, over the government of all nations. Constance Cumbey in her book, *The Hidden Dangers Of The Rainbow*, says of the Great Invocation:

"The Great Invocation was first given out and used in 1945 and since that date has become familiar to millions of people all over the world, and is used daily by them. This world prayer expresses truths central to all major religions ... Since it was first given out, the Invocation has spread to all parts of the globe, using every possible means of communication (the translation from the original English has been made into 52 foreign languages) ... The Festival of the Christ, and World Invocation Day, is the Festival in which Christ represents humanity in the sight of God ... Since 1952, it has been observed as World Invocation Day ... The Invocation continues to be featured in the press on many occasions in many countries of the world. As each year passes, the extent and range of the coverage increases. It is appearing in daily newspapers, church and general magazines, college and cultural publications, meeting notices and programs ... Coverage in the press reaches a peak each year at the time of World Invocation Day ... One of the most encouraging responses to the Invocation is from the churches and religious groups of many denominations who request supplies of Invocation cards and leaflets for distribution to congregations and group members, to men's clubs, youth groups, women's alliances, etc ... The Great Invocation was first used in 1945, the same year the United Nations was founded ... Twenty years later a leaflet was issued showing how the Great Invocation could be used by men and women of goodwill to strengthen the United Nations ..."

As Mrs. Cumbey's book brings out, millions of Christians are being deceived into praying the Devil's prayer. To Mrs. Cumbey's warning, we add the words of the Apostle Paul: "And then shall that Wicked be revealed, whom the Lord shall consume with the spirit of his mouth, and shall destroy with the brightness of his coming: Even him, whose coming is after the working of Satan with all power and signs and lying wonders,

And with all deceivableness of unrighteousness in them that perish; because they receive not the love of the truth, that they might be saved. And for this cause God shall send them strong delusion, that they should believe a lie: That they all might be damned who believed not the truth, but had pleasure in unrighteousness" (II Thess. 2:8-12).

In August 1983, a full-page, paid advertisement appeared in *Newsweek, Time, U.S. News and World Report,* and other of the most widely read weekly news magazines in the world. This ad featured a picture of another Hindu guru called "His Holiness Maharishi Mahesh Yogi" (founder of Transcendental Meditation).

The headline reads: "Governments Invited To Solve Their Problems."

"The World Government Of The Age Of Enlightenment Announces its readiness to solve the problems of any government regardless of the magnitude and nature of the problem — political, economic, social, or religious; and irrespective of its system — capitalism, communism, socialism, democracy, or dictatorship. Governments are invited to contact the World Government of the Age of Enlightenment to solve their problems on the basis of cost reimbursement after the target is reached. 1983 can be the year of fulfillment for every government."

The ad continues to promise autonomy for all governments, with the added guarantee that all internal and external problems will be solved, and a new age of peace, plenty, harmony and religious fulfillment will permeate the earth. Evidently, Mahesh Yogi is attempting to become the New

Age messiah himself, and the ad closes with the following benediction:

"With the blessing of Guru Dev, life on earth now is on the doorstep of the perpetual sunshine of the Age of Enlightenment."

From *Time* Magazine, the December 19, 1983, issue we find the following advertisement:

"Maharishi Technology of the Unified Field — Solving Problems of Governments – Creating Ideal Civilization of Earth — A Taste of Utopia — Dec. 17-Jan. 6, 1984 — The World Government of the age of enlightenment offered last month to solve the problems of all governments. In the same wave of inspiration, Maharishi International University has now planned to give a sample taste of Utopia to all mankind. Seven thousand experts in the Maharishi Technology of the Unified Field will assemble at MIU from December 17 to January 6 to collectively create a strong influence of coherence and positivity in the whole world. This unique demonstration of global coherence, originating from one place and reaching all parts of the world, will inspire governments to follow this example in their own countries and create a group of experts in the Maharishi sociology of the Unified Field so that negative trends do not arise in the country, law and order are spontaneously maintained, and administration becomes simple, effective, free from problems, and free from the elements of fear and punishment. Real freedom will be enjoyed by the people and by the government. The sweet taste of Utopia comes as the supreme gift of the Silver Jubilee celebrations of Maharishi's Worldwide Transcendental Meditation Movement, 1958 to 1983. Maharishi declared 1983 to be the 'Year of the Unified Field.' Now, 1984 will be welcomed as the 'Year of the Unified Field Based Civilization.' "

In the last decade, the New Age Church has really come into view nationwide. Here is an article that demonstrates how the New Age Churches are proliferating and growing rapidly. Minneapolis — December 18, 1983 "New Age Churches Growing Vigorously. They Blend Some Christian Beliefs With Ideas From Other Religions."

"The Rev. Donald Clark stood amid swirling snow in the cavernous sanctuary, still under construction, and talked about the growth of his Unity Church in Golden Valley. A decade ago its beliefs were considered exotic by conventional standards, and the congregation numbered only 125. But today, fresh concrete and new steel girders attest to growing acceptance of the church's unusual tenets and its efforts to accommodate a burgeoning congregation of more than 500.

"That growth is parallel with an expansion nationwide of what have come to be called New Age churches, such as Unity. Although New Age churches generally follow the teachings of Jesus Christ, titles in Unity's book store downstairs reflect decided differences between mainline Christianity and the New Age approach: 'The Aquarian Gospel of Jesus Christ,' 'Reincarnation: Karma and Resurrection,' 'Studies of the Human Aura,' 'Seven Schools of Yoga,' 'The Gift of Healing,' 'UFOs: Key to Earth's Destiny,' and 'Tofu Madness.' Locally, there are perhaps 2,000 serious students of New Age religion and 20,000 dabblers, said Doris Finke, who calls herself the great-grandmother of the movement locally and who teaches 'A course in Miracles' at Unity. Nationally, New Age religion is a 'large and serious movement' with a following of about a million people in North American Religions in Evanston, IL. The movement is eclectic and resists easy definition. It has no dogmas, liturgies or structures such as those that readily identify Lutherans or Roman Catholics. But its followers generally believe in reincarnation and spiritual healing and that human beings are, like Jesus Christ, both human and divine, said Carol Parrish, a New Age teacher based in Oklahoma, who has a Twin Cities following of hundreds of people. "It's almost like an underground, because people aren't aware it's as prevalent as it is,' Clark said. Yet Unity Metaphysical Bookstore sells $30,000 worth of tapes, books and pamphlets a year, and 15,000 people in the Twin Cities area subscribe to the 'Daily Word' published at Unity Village, the national center for 400 Unity churches nationwide. 'New Age people do not subscribe to an anthropomorphic God . . . an old man with a white beard, sitting on a cloud,' Clark said. 'Rather, they view God as a universal intelligence and presence pervading humankind.'"

Here is a 10-page newsletter from a New Age organization called "Organization of Psychic-Research Associates."

This publication, dated July 1983, announced a New Age Meeting, and the headline reads, "Rainbow Promise Holds True: Dream Conference Prospers."

The newletter reported a membership of 426 with 27 new members, and it contains all the New Age doctrines, verbiage, and occult propaganda, including meditation, New Age Music, Tarot, Astrology, etc.

A message from the president of the organization reads in part: "Being president is like being the top of a mount; it's only as secure as the rocks below you. You, the members of OPRA, form the bedrock on which the other officers and I can work. We depend on your support for the projects and programs we introduce . . . During the summer months when some of the routine and special events slack off, share the load with us by volunteering your time, talents, gifts and service. We need your help with telephoning, mailing, typing, bookkeeping, news reporting, editing, layout, paste-up and hosting of study groups. We need committee leaders and members for membership, conference planning, publicity, advertising, by-laws, ethics, education and research . . . volunteer now; the best teacher is experience. And don't forget the cosmic law: What you send out comes back — many times over. OPRA is at an all-time high . . . We have a place to meet, capital to work with, enthusiastic officers and a membership of 426 . . . we have the opportunity to offer more services and programs than ever before. We want your ideas, and we need your help."

Now where is this thriving New Age organization located? Seattle? Los Angeles? New York? Chicago? No, none of these places. It is in Midwest City, an affluent suburb of Oklahoma City, where one of the largest Air Force Supply Centers in the world, Tinker Field, is located, just ten miles from our office. And similar newletters from other New Age chapters like this one are mailed to us almost daily from all over the United States.

A former Mason dropped by our office to leave a copy of a Masonic magazine, titled, *The New Age*. And inasmuch as most of the terminology of the Masons parallels the verbiage of the New Age Movement, many unsuspecting Masons may be led to believe it is a good thing.

How do we identify New Age organizations? Here's a helpful article on the New Age by Gregg Levoy, *Minneapolis Tribune*, December 18, 1983.

"Remember the 'hidden pictures' in children's magazines? In what appeared to be an ordinary scene with a lake and woods and farmhouse was 'hidden' a pitchfork, a toothbrush, a lightbulb. Once you knew what to look for, they were plainly there. You wondered how you missed them before.

"On a shelf by the door in Arnold's Bar and Grill on Eighth Street is a clutter of tabloids all published in Cincinnati: INNER QUEST, NEW LIFE-STYLES, GREATER CINCINNATI RESOURCE DIRECTORY, EAST/WEST CENTER NEWS-LETTER, DISCOVERY CENTER. They're resource guides for a revolution most people have missed because they haven't been looking for it.

"That's understandable. The revolution has been called 'The Movement That Has No Name' by Marilyn Ferguson, author of *The Aquarian Conspiracy*, one of the first researchers to attempt mapping out this phenomenon many people are simply calling 'The New Age.'

"In his bestseller *Megatrends*, writer John Naisbitt enumerates changes taking place in society, which he says are actually the symptoms of the New Age: decentralization of authority and decision-making; authentic and personal religious experience instead of bureaucratized religion; long-range versus short-range business values; self-help instead of institutional help; and a movement from hierarchies to networks.

"These values are not only getting into the mainstream" says Peggy Taylor, editor of the 50,000 circulation *New Age* magazine. "They're becoming the mainstream.

"Sociological method has fallen short in determining how many people are involved in this evolving mainstream.

"William McCready of the National Opinion Research Corporation says, 'If you try to gauge it by membership in groups, you won't see it. Because they aren't much for joining. The people involved in this inner search are hard to pin down statistically.'

"Some polls taken in recent years may prove more enlightening.

"A Gallup poll in 1978 reported that 10 million Americans alone were engaged in some aspect of Eastern religion, and nine million in spiritual healing.

"A recent Yankelovich, Skelly and White poll showed 80 percent of the respondents strongly interested in 'an inner search for meaning.'

"The New Age is a synthesis, author Ferguson explains, of the social activism of the '60s and the 'consciousness revolution' and human potential movement of the '70s: social transformation resulting from personal transformation — change from the inside out. Change, goes the New Age attitude, can only be facilitated, not decreed.

"The change, Ferguson says, is characterized by the intergrating of science and mysticism, technology and art, business and human need, mind and body. Old divisive ways of thinking are being given some connective tissue.

"If one is looking for conventional symbols of change or a new kind of religiousness, it won't readily be found. A partial list of some of the disciplines embodying the New Age spirit will reveal this. They aren't exactly the same old pitchforks and toothbrushes."

Another item of deception used by the New Age Movement is the Rainbow.

New Agers have adopted the rainbow as their sign of the coming Luciferian millennium.

Constance Cumbey says, "Although the rainbow seems to be only a colored arc of light refracted through raindrops, to both Christians and New Agers it has a deep meaning. According to the Bible, the rainbow is symbolic of God's everlasting covenant that He would never again destroy the earth by a flood. However, the New Age Movement uses rainbows to signify their building of the Rainbow bridge (antahkarana) between man and Lucifer who, they say, is the over-soul. New Agers place small rainbow decals on their automobiles and book stores as a signal to others in the Movement. Some people, of course, use the rainbow as a decoration, unaware of the growing popular acceptance of its occult meaning and the hidden dangers."

The New Age Movement is growing. Its propaganda is receiving ever-increasing dissemination. The main part of their message that is attracting the most attention is the promise that a messiah is coming soon to bring in a golden age of peace, plenty and prosperity. It does not make any difference whether you are a Christian, a Buddhist, a Hindu, a Humanist, a Jew or a Moslem, because your Lord is just one of many Masters, and the greatest Master of all, the christ of all religions, is coming soon. You don't have to be born again, confess your sins, change your lifestyle — just get in step and help them work to get this message to all the world.

Today, in almost every city, there are training centers and seminars being conducted for New Age thinking. Even though some of them may not promote overt occult teaching, the key to their New Age Movement connection is that they want to rearrange your thinking. They want you to discover your inner power; to rid yourself of self-defeating moral codes. Many Christians who have been forewarned have refused to attend these New Age thinking seminars, even if it meant losing their jobs.

Offices for Lucis Trust, located at 866 United Nations Plaza in New York, display dozens of attractive booklets for world travelers who come to the United Nations. We have a large number of these in our possession, and they all promote New Age propaganda and most of them have The Great Invocation.

The New Age Movement uses the United

Nations as a propaganda carrier to other nations. The June 1983 Tara Center publication titled *Update On The Reappearance Of The Christ* states on page 4: "Benjamin Creme has predicted that the United Nations will be one of the important organizations through which world hunger will be eradicated."

Although the New Age Movement's christ did not appear in 1982 as announced, Benjamin Creme reported in the June 1983 edition of Tara's newsletter: "Maitreya still awaits an invitation from the media through which to present Himself to the world ... Could it be this Pentecost? If Maitreya were discovered in time, then certainly it could be ..."

While the world media has failed to cooperate in announcing the New Age's messiah, the permeation of New Age occult propaganda continues to increase at all levels — religious, economic, political and social. Admittedly, the New Age Movement has as much right to establish chapters and communicate its own particular religion as any other religion, including the Catholic Church or Protestant churches.

However, as Christians we have an obligation to reveal to all people that the christ the New Agers are proclaiming is not Jesus Christ, but rather the Antichrist.

The New Age Movement is based on a spiritual hierarchy of illumined ones, ascended masters, who will at the right time reveal their christ to mankind. The New Age Movement believes in reincarnation, evolution, astrology, mind control, that man can become god, worship of Lucifer, the oneness of all religions and that Jesus Christ was just one of many messiahs the Masters have sent into the world.

The warning against all evil, satanic movements is given in I John 4:1-3:

"Beloved, believe not every spirit, but try the spirits whether they are of God: because many false prophets are gone out into the world. Hereby know ye the Spirit of God: Every spirit that confesseth that Jesus Christ is come in the flesh is of God: And every spirit that confesseth not that Jesus Christ is come in the flesh is not of God: and this is that spirit of antichrist, whereof ye have heard that it should come; and even now already is it in the world."

3

NEW MONEY FOR 1984-85

Another exciting development in the Orwellian concept of 1984 is the possible introduction of a new currency for seven nations, including the United States. That the new currency fits into the prophetic picture of "Big Brother" and the coming antichrist system will be quite evident.

Money has played a leading role in the rise and fall of empires.

King Nebuchadnezzar gathered all the gold and silver from the known world to build Babylon and idols to his false gods.

Persia established provinces and an extensive tax system to maintain the huge Persian army and build cities of marble.

Alexander took over the Persian tax system and placed his own tax collectors in all the nations he conquered.

Rome collected taxes from world trade and commerce.

Spain sent armies to the Americas in search of gold, and much of this can be found in churches in Toledo, Madrid, Seville and other Spanish cities.

Napoleon lost his bid for a world empire when the Rothschilds of Europe double-crossed him and withdrew financial backing.

Nations with the best economy and soundest money usually win wars.

Jesus said of money, "Render therefore unto Caesar the things which are Caesar's; and unto God the things that are God's" (Matthew 22:21).

God's work in both government and church must be supported.

In Israel, government was supported by taxes, and the priesthood was supported by tithes and offerings. The principal unit of exchange was the shekel, which was equal to one-half ounce of gold or one-half ounce of silver. The gold shekel was worth from five to ten dollars, while the silver shekel was worth about sixty-five cents.

Today, the paper shekel in Israel is worth about two cents. The deflated value of the shekel is due to inflation and the fact that there is no gold or silver backing of the shekel in Israel.

The international monetary unit in banking, trade or commerce is the United States' dollar. Since the United States can no longer back up the dollar with gold or silver reserves, the value of the dollar is based solely on the wealth of our nation and the stability of our government.

During periods of inflation, uncertain government changes, war or international crises, and other factors which may affect the course of our political system or our economy, the value of the dollar fluctuates greatly on the international market and the price of gold and silver rises.

We quote from an article by Maxwell Newton that appeared in the September 19, 1982 edition of the *New York Post*:

"The United States was once a major economic power in the world, possessing vast investments abroad. By 1976, these new investments amounted to just over $80 billion. Yet, ... as a result of huge current account deficits in the years 1976 through 1983, the U.S. will have dissipated all these investments by some time in the first half of 1984. In the years 1977, 1978, 1979, 1980, 1981, 1982, and the first half of 1983, the U.S. recorded a cumulative deficit on current accounts of $50 billion. This reduced the net international investment position from over $80 billion in 1976 to about $30 billion today and to a prospective negative amount in the first half of 1984, as the U.S. is confidently forecast to record a further massive current account deficit on the order of $40 billion between the middle of 1983 and middle of 1984. How has this appalling loss of power and influence by the U.S. come about? There are several reasons:

"1. The most obvious is the Great Inflation this country has suffered since 1975. Between 1975 and July 1983, consumer prices rose 85 percent, drastically weakening the economic power of American industry; raising effective rates of taxation so that corporations and individuals had a drastically declining surplus of savings to invest.

"2. Another major reason for the drastic loss of overseas wealth by the U.S. was the extraordinary growth of government spending, which gobbled up the nation's resources and dissipated them in an unprecedented explosion of spending on social programs, including Social Security, Welfare, Medicare and the like. As governments gobbled up resources to provide handouts to Americans in return for votes, there were less and less savings available to finance investment and indeed there was less and less of anything available to finance investment and indeed there was less and less of anything available to satisfy the insatiable demands by governments for resources to provide handouts. During the last half of the 1970's, resources to finance the massive expansion of Handout America that occurred were found by means of a massive confiscation of wealth. Between 1976 and 1982, the 'real' value of bonds fell by one-half and the 'real' value of stocks fell by about one-third. This was a huge confiscation of wealth. It was brought about by inflationary finance provided by the Federal Reserve. This inflationary finance, in the form of excessive growth of money, promoted massive inflation and, in this inflation, the accumulated savings of millions of Americans, represented by stocks and bonds, were cut in half.

"3. By 1982, the financial markets were in revolt and they have remained so ever since. They expressed their revulsion of what had happened to them by demanding high 'real' interest rates ...

One consequence of the 'revolt of the financial markets' was that a major source of resources to finance excessive growth of government spending was denied to politicians. It was no longer possible to carry out *de facto* confiscation of wealth by means of inflationary finance. As a result, high interest rates meant that the U.S. experienced the phenomenon of the 'strong dollar' and this in turn meant the high balance of payment deficits we are experiencing, leading to the massive liquidation of American overseas investments... In this way, the issue of facing the true nature of the crisis of social spending could be avoided for a further period of time — by devouring the nation's overseas patrimony."

In essence what the huge federal deficits and the money policies have done is equivalent to cashing in your savings accounts without lowering the balance of your checking account. However, the government deficits continue to loom larger and larger.

The question is, where do the Federal Reserve and our federal economic advisors go next?

By cashing in on investments, inflation and high interest rates have been subdued. Tax reduction, especially in the business sector, has also helped to slowly turn our internal business barometer upward. However, many financial observers believe that unprecedented deficits will again force the government to corner the money market in order to pay the interest on the runaway debt. Consequently, inflation will once again increase and interest rates will accelerate once more, and the business recovery will end, bringing with it the threat of another economic crash.

As long as two years ago, some observers reported that a new currency had already been printed for use when the crash came and our government canceled the national debt and issued new money. These past rumors are given revived credence through the circulation of a letter signed by Ron Paul, congressman from the 32nd District in Texas. Congressman Paul is on the Committee on Banking, Finance and Urban Affairs. The letter is shown as being addressed to Mr. Charles T. Roberts, executive vice president, Hull State Bank, Hull, Texas:

"Dear Mr. Roberts:

"Because you have written to me in the past about our monetary system, I thought you would be interested in the latest development from the Federal Reserve System, in a closed briefing for the Members of the House banking committee on November 2, representatives of the Bureau of Engraving and Printing, the Federal Reserve and Secret Service described plans for making changes in Federal Reserve notes beginning in 1985. In the next two months, the Secretary of the Treasury will be making decisions on the specific changes to be made in the currency. The government maintains that the Secretary has power to make any such changes without the prior approval of Congress. These changes, which will probably include taggents, security threads, and colors, and may include holograms, diffraction gratings, or watermarks, will be made in coordination with six other nations: Canada, Britain, Japan, Australia, West Germany and Switzerland. Japan, for example, will begin recalling its present currency in November 1984 and have it nearly completed within six months. The activities are being coordinated by the Advanced Anti-counterfeiting Deterrent Committee set up in 1978. The Committee has held many meetings over the past five years, the last one in Australia four weeks ago. According to the government, the only reason for the currency changes is to deter counterfeiting. Although it was admitted by one spokesman in the group that there would have to be a call-in of our present currency for the new currency to work, the spokesmen for the government were adamant in saying that there was no other motive for a currency exchange, such as exchange controls or flushing out of the underground economy. I believe that we need a new money, not new colors on old money. That is why I've introduced H.R. 4226 to provide for the minting of gold and silver coins as provided in the Constitution. If you would like further information about these matters, please write to me at my office in Washington."

We called Congressman Paul's office to verify that he had written the letter because there have been incidents where such letters have been forged. However, we were assured by his secretary that the letter was authentic and the facts were accurate.

Congressman Paul, as a member of the Congressional Committee on Banking, Finance, and Urban Affairs, as well as being the ranking Republican on the Subcommittee on Consumer Affairs and Coinage, should know what he is talking about.

According to Congressman Paul, the following items are worthy of note:

1. The new money will be issued by the Federal Reserve System.

2. As we have previously reported, the different denominations ($1.00, $5.00, $10.00, $20.00, etc.) will be issued in various colors.

3. The new money will have diffraction gratings and possibly holograms. This probably means computer code marks as the computerized checkout counters operate on the holograph system.

4. This will not be just U.S. currency, but it will also be for Canada, Britain, Japan, Australia, West Germany and Switzerland. Counting the United States, that would make seven nations. A common currency of the world's most industrialized nations could provide strong incentives for the new dollar to become a truly world, computerized currency. This could also raise new possibilities of the United States becoming Revived Babylon of Jeremiah 51, 52, and Revelation 18.

5. The sole reason given for new money is to deter counterfeiting, but this would appear to be rather absurd. Counterfeiting is not that much of a problem today with all the Internal Revenue tax contols and sophisticated detecting methods and devices.

6. Canada, Britian, Japan, Australia, West Ger-

many and Switzerland will begin recalling their money in November 1984 in preparation for replacing their currency with their versions of the new money planned for the United States. According to Congressman Paul, the United States will follow sometime in 1985.

7.   A six-month's period will be granted for the exchange of the old green currency. After the six months have expired, the old currency will become worthless. In spite of claims to the contrary, the new money system will give the governments of all seven nations stronger control of earnings and taxable incomes. Thousands who have hidden money not reported may be indicted for tax evasion if they attempt to exchange the old currency for new money.

8. Governments can rob their citizenry of material wealth in ways other than at the end of a gun. As previously noted, through politically induced inflation, our government reduced the 'real' extent of the national debt and robbed people of their earnings and savings from the years 1975 through 1981. If the dollar is to remain as a unit of world trade and commerce, the national debt must be eliminated, since it is now so huge and the interest so great it cannot be reduced. The basis for the exchange rate between the old currency and the new money is not yet known. We must suspect that behind this new money program there will be an attempt to erase it.

These reported plans in the world's basic currency system are just another link in the financial chain that will one day bind all nations to the Antichrist system. "... that no man might buy or sell, save he that had the mark, or the name of the beast, or the number of his name" (Rev 13:17).

Many financial observers believe that if new U.S. money is issued, or if huge federal deficits continue, that gold may increase in value to $4,000 an ounce. After World War II, the United States owned 60 percent of the world's gold supply, and most of our gold was stored under government protection at Fort Knox, Kentucky.

Our paper money, at one time, was issued with the notation that it could be redeemed in gold or silver.

The first International Monetary Fund conference, held in 1944, was under the direction of Harry Dexter White, a member of the Council on Foreign Relations and an undercover Soviet espionage agent. It was at that first IMF conference that it was decided to move the gold from Fort Knox to other countries. This was done through foreign aid and the expense of maintaining American forces overseas.

The United States would redeem it's paper money in gold at $36 to $42 an ounce, while the same gold would be sold on the foreign market for several hundred dollars an ounce. Once our gold was gone, the price of gold immediately rose to $800 an ounce. Even though it is now selling at about half that amount, Richard Hughes, who is the president of the Southwest Radio Church Society of Canada, and who is in the gold mining business, believes that the price of gold will soar above $3,000 an ounce. Almost all financial advisors are bullish on buying gold and silver.

The *McAlvany Intelligence Advisor* of November 1983 stated:

"A panic washout could take gold as low as $340 to $360 an ounce and silver to the $8.00 to $8.50 range over the next few weeks. This writer simply views this pullback as an excellent buying opportunity in long-term bull market which should take gold to $1,500 to $2,000 an ounce and silver to $60 to $75 by 1986. War, inflation and banking crises will push the metal sharply higher in 1984 and 1986."

If the United States had retained its gold, then there would be no economic crises. But what has happened was planned 40 years ago in 1944.

Former FBI agent Dan Smoot wrote in his report dated October 21, 1963:

"This is the first time in living memory that we've had to borrow money from foreign governments ... which merely postpones the day when our fiscal chickens come home to roost ... How did this happen? It was planned at the United Nations Monetary and Financial conference, held in Bretton Woods, New Hampshire, from July 1 to July 22, 1944. Harry Dexter White was head of the American delegation to the Bretton Woods conference. In 1944 the United States held 60% of the world's known gold reserve, and was the dominant economic and financial power. Hence, Harry Dexter White, officially designated as principal spokesman for the United States, controlled the Bretton Woods Conference. White, a member of the Council on Foreign Relations, was an undercover Soviet espionage agent ... Harry Dexter White's Bretton Woods Conference of 1944 set

the basic policies which our government has followed ... These policies were intended to accomplish four major objectives:

"1. Strip the United States of the great gold
reserve by giving gold away to other nations.

"2. Build up the industrial capacity of other
nations, at our expense, to eliminate American
productive superiority.

"3. Take world markets (and much of the
American domestic market) away from American
producers until capitalistic America would no
longer dominate world trade.

"4. Entwine American affairs — economic, political, cultural, social, educational and even religious — with those of other nations until the
United States could no longer have an independent policy but would become an interdependent
link in a worldwide socialist chain."

| | | |

It appears more than coincidental that every
one of these objectives outlined by Smoot more
than twenty years ago have been obtained.

President Kennedy stated at the meeting of the
International Monetary Fund on September 30,
1963, to representatives from 102 nations:

"Twenty years ago, when the architects of
these institutions met to design an international
banking structure, the economic life of the world
was polarized in an overwhelming and even alarming measure on the United States. So were the
world's monetary reserves. The United States
had the only open capital in the world apart from
that of Switzerland. Sixty percent of the gold re-

serves of the world were here in the United States ... There was a need for redistribution of the financial resources of the world ... This has come about. It did not come about by chance BUT BY CONSCIOUS AND DELIBERATE AND RESPONSIBLE PLANNING" (emphasis added).

The International Monetary Fund is still the medium being used to bring about the demise of the dollar and the present economic system, and it would appear that the new money that is scheduled to appear in 1985 will serve as only a transitional currency.

Since 1944 the IMF has planned an international monetary system based on computerized transfers of electronic currency. Although the realization of the mechanics of this goal did not become apparent until the 60s, this was the intent from the beginning.

We quote from a recent *Reuter's News Release* from England:

"Proposals for changes in borrowing rules, likely to have an impact on the world's monetary system, are being examined by the executive board of the International Monetary Fund ... The board is also considering making more money available to countries in the form of the fund's own international currency, the Special Drawing Right (SDR). The poorer countries favor such a step, while the United States has generally opposed it because of its possible inflationary impact. The two proposed changes are expected to be key issues when the IMF and the World Bank hold their joint annual meeting ... "

Through the IMF, billions of dollars have been

loaned to nations like Brazil and Mexico. These nations are not financially able to repay these loans.

A new money system that would eventually be based on Special Drawing Rights would spell the final doom for the dollar and erase the international debt, just as the new dollar in 1985 may result in the liquidation of our U.S. national debt.

Quoted as one reason for the evolution of a new money is the increasing problems of domestic banks.

We quote from a September 19, 1983, *New York Times* news release:

"Almost 600 banks in the United States are in deep financial trouble because of bad loans ... This is the highest level ever recorded by the FDIC, officials said, far above the previous high reached shortly after the 1973-1975 recession. Banks on the problem list are generally characterized by unsafe, unsound, or other seriously unsatisfactory conditions and carry a relatively high possibility of failure of insolvency ... "

Another reason for the transitional dollar that is scheduled to appear in 1985 is that paper money simply does not fit into either our domestic "Big Brother" environment, or the even "bigger international brother's" social order that is looming on the horizon. Money is simply going to be as archaic as the Model-T Ford.

We quote from a *New York Daily News* story dated September 22, 1983:

"A plan to allow the city's 500,000 welfare recipients to use an electronically coded card to get monthly payments from banks or check-cashing outlets, instead of by mail, was unveiled yesterday. The system, used since November 1981 on an experimental basis by 10,000 welfare families on the upper West Side, also allows food stamp recipients to get food stamps directly, eliminating a need to mail notices... Jack Deacy, spokesman for Human Resources Administration, said the plan was developed to reduce the $800,000 that the city loses annually because of forged and stolen welfare checks. He said that under the new system, to be phased in citywide beginning next fall, welfare recipients will be issued photo-identification cards ... The card will be run through a machine to verify the cardholder's identity and how much money or food stamps he or she is entitled to ... Deacy said the city would pay $6 million to a private firm to set up the computer network and would pay banks and check cashing outlets $1.50 for each transaction... Deacy said, 'Since the experiment began on the upper West Side we've handled about 350,000 transactions without one report of theft, forgery or fraud.' "

Jesus said that as it was in the days of Noah, so it would be when He came again.

In the days of Noah, crime and violence filled the earth and the thoughts of men were only evil continually.

When the elderly, lame, blind, widows and orphans cannot obtain help without being robbed of their pitiful little assistance checks, then we have indeed gone backward to the days of Noah. And this is why mankind is turning to computerized machines to render services and decisions from a strictly amoral position — being neither good nor evil of themselves.

We quote from page 59 of the December 5, 1983 edition of *U.S. News And World Report*:

"Never temperamental, always on time, untiringly efficient, Epistle scans the boss's mail, culls out important letters and highlights significant facts before the executive arrives. Epistle is no ordinary secretary. It is a robot being developed by IBM — part of a fast-growing breed of devices that can think and reason something like the human brain ... Already, computers have been built to carry out mental feats that are astonishing in their human-like characteristics... Technology is changing the computer from a fantastically fast calculating machine to a device that can see, touch, smell, recognize spoken commands and answer in plain English,' says Melvin W. Siegle, head of the Intelligent Sensors Laboratory at Carnegie-Melton University's Robot Institute. Such machines mull over problems, make judgements, acquire additional learning when necessary, and eventually may even acquire emotions — declaring their likes and dislikes to their human counterparts ... If artifical intelligences can be created at all, there is little reason to believe that they could not lead swiftly to the construction of superintelligences."

This article continues to report that computer and electronic experts are concerned that the human race may lose control of its own destiny to artificial intelligence.

Dr. Robert Jastrow, founder of Goddard Space Center, in his book, *The Enchanted Loom,* expressed the view that man of necessity will create a super brain to govern the world.

On page 159, he says:

"Most people would say that a computer can never be a living organism, because it has no feelings or emotions; it does not eat, or move, or grow and it is made of metal and plastic rather than flesh, bone and muscle. Most of these attributes can easily be built into computers if they were desired ... I believe that in a larger cosmic perspective, going beyond the earth and its biological creatures, the true attributes of intelligent life will be seen to be those that are shared by man and computer— a response to stimuli, absorption of information about the world ... The brain that possesses these attributes may be made of water and carbon-chain molecules, and housed in a fragile shell of bone, as our brain is; or it may be made of metallic silicon, housed in plastic; but if it reacts to the world around it, and grows through experience, it is alive."

An article on page 86 of the December 5, 1983 *U.S. News And World Report* titled "Time To Throw Away Your Checkbook," brings out that within ten years we will not need checkbooks, wallets, coins or dollar bills. All financial transactions involving buying, working or selling, will be done with a plastic card with code marks and numbers on it.

So, beyond the new money that, according to Congressman Ron Paul of the House Committee on Finance and Urban Affairs, is due to arrive by 1985, there is a cashless economic order on the horizon where your own personal name will mean nothing.

Without a code mark and a number, the individual becomes an economic non-entity.

According to Dr. Jastrow, this new order may be governed by an artificially created super-intelligence.

"And he had power to give life unto the image of the beast, that the image of the beast should both speak, and cause that as many as would not worship the image of the beast should be killed. And he causeth all, both small and great, rich and poor, free and bond, to receive a mark in their right hand, or in their foreheads: And that no man might buy or sell, save he that had the mark, or the name of the beast, or the number of his name" (Rev 13: 17).

4

THE BIO–COMPUTER — MAN'S MESSIAH?

The item that dominates the world's news media today is rampaging computer technology.

Computer scientists contend that within ten years the computer will control mankind's total being. This awesome power that is destined to guide the destiny of the human race is causing many experts to wonder if man is not now in the process of creating his own god.

Amazingly, it is not primarily the leaders and spokesmen for religion that are expressing concern, but rather the computer makers themselves. Some are attempting to justify the neo-godly aspects of the new computers by explaining that it really does not make any difference, because God is in the computer.

For example, we quote from page 94 of the

book, *The Fifth Generation*, published in 1983: "As the philosopher and logician Alfred North Whitehead observed, God is in the details."

On page 40 of the May, 1984 edition of *Science* appears a lengthy article titled "Computer Worship."

This article begins with a full-page color picture of a computer on the altar in a church with a beam of light from heaven illuminating its presence for the worship service. The authors present the claim by computer experts that in the future students will not need to master reading, writing or arithmetic. All that will be needed to equip young people to meet life's challenges is to learn how to operate the new generation of computers.

The Psalmist said that though he ascended into heaven, or descended into Hell, God was there.

The Apostle Paul said that in God we move and have our being.

Today, the same can be said of the computer.

A computer controls the traffic lights through which we must pass on our way to work.

It is a computer that tells us when we can go and when we must stop.

A computer controls our banking, our working, our buying and selling.

Modern man fears a computer failure more than God's wrath against sin.

Even in Christian organizations the computer controls communications.

At the 1984 convention of National Religious Broadcasters we attended a computer workshop. A spokesman for one of the larger organizations stated that their mailing list was computerized into 36 categories.

A computer determines the type of letter the donor receives, the kind of envelope, the gift asked for, the design on the stationery and how often each person is to be contacted.

A vision of the perfect computerized man of the Fifth Generation is described in an article titled, "What Next? A World Of Communications Wonders," page 59 of the April 9, 1984 edition of *U.S. News And World Report*: "A phone in every pocket, a computer in every home: That and more await consumers as astonishing Information Age techniques start to pay off. A global telecommunications revolution is poised to bring astonishing changes to virtually every American — especially anyone who picks up a telephone, switches on a television set or logs into a computer. Growing out of the marriage of communications links with modern computers, the new technologies are spreading lightning fast. Experts say that the upheaval won't end until anyone, anywhere can reach out and touch anyone else — instantly and effortlessly through electronics. Among the extraordinary possibilities in store for consumers by the end of this century:

"*The standard telephone console will become the only computer terminal most people will need. Text and pictures will be viewed on a video screen attached to the phone, and additional data will be delivered as electronically synthesized speech. Phone users also will be able to see who is calling before answering.

"*Combining laser optics and computers, three-dimensional holographic images will bring TV features into living rooms with almost lifelike clarity.

"*Automobiles will have not only telephones as standard equipment but also satellite navigation devices to pinpoint a vehicle's location and guide the driver to any destination.

"*Automatic-translation devices will allow people to insert a text in English and have it delivered in minutes to a distant point in Japanese, Arabic or one of many other languages.

"Already, the conduits of yesterday — copper wires, radio signals, ground antennas and even electricity itself — are giving way to glass fibers, microwaves, satellites, laser beams and the pulsating digital languages of computers. The economic potential of such unprecedented changes in communications technology is practically limitless: Sales of hardware alone reached 60 billion dollars in 1983 . . . Like a summer vine that shoots out in every direction without a discernable pattern, the telecommunications grip also is spreading uncontrollably. Never before have so many individuals and organizations been able to interact on such a vast scale. By the end of the century, electronic information technology will have transformed American business, manufacturing, school, family, political and home life . . . says William McGowan, chairman of MCI Communications Corporation: 'Telecommunications is one business today in which you don't need losers to have winners. There is enough for everybody. The instruments in this sweeping electronic upheaval — computers, electronic links and video technologies — are the interlocking parts of a communications network undreamed of only a decade ago.' "

At Babel man became too intelligent and resourceful for his own good, so God disrupted communications — He changed the common language into many so that if a man asked for a brick he was given mortar.

Today, man's new god, the computer, is reversing the communications breakdown.

Your computer will soon be able to translate instantly what anyone speaking in a foreign language is saying.

It is clearly prophesied in Revelation 13 that everyone in the world will fall down and worship the image of Antichrist, and now computerized communications will transmit images of the world's political leaders, or leader, in three dimensions into your own living room.

We read in Daniel 12:4 that in the last days knowledge, travel and communication — will greatly increase.

Again, we look to the computer for the fulfillment of this prophecy.

In the future all commerce and banking will be done via the computer terminal and every man must have his own computer code mark and number as we read in Revelation 13:17, "And that no man might buy or sell, save he that had the mark, or the name of the beast, or the number of his name."

Another interesting scripture that may have a relation to our subject is Revelation 6:5,6. "And when he had opened the third seal, I heard the third beast say, Come and see. And I beheld, and lo a black horse; and he that sat on him had a pair of balances in his hand. And I heard a voice in the midst of the four beasts say, A measure of wheat for a penny, and three measures of barley for a penny; and see thou hurt not the oil and the wine."

This prophecy initially refers to either the worthlessness of money, or high inflation that will be prevalent during the coming Great Tribulation. One penny represented an average day's wages at the time John wrote the Revelation.

The second part of the prophecy has reference to medical care as oil and wine is not to be hurt, or made scarce. Oil and wine were the principal medicines used during the time of Christ.

We read in Luke 10:34 that the good Samaritan poured oil and wine on the wounds of the man injured by robbers.

Medical care is one of the services that men and women demand most today. The elderly have Medicare, and almost everyone else has health insurance of some kind. Many nations have government-sponsored medical programs, and yet doctor and hospital fees continue to increase until a heavy burden has been placed on society that is difficult to bear.

Now we are informed that Dr. Computer is not only going to be a better physician but also much less costly. The computer, according to medical sources, is destined to play an increasing role in medical services. Some computers are even now making diagnoses, writing prescriptions, and recommending courses of treatment. Needless to say, a second opinion is not necessary.

A bulletin from the *The Research Institute*

Of America dated April 1984 states: "Computers are playing an even larger role as diagnostic tools ... Computers are invading doctors' offices in growing numbers. Cooperation between medical doctors and computer scientists has become a rapidly growing area of specialization."

The article continues to attest that in diagnosing diseases in 500 individuals, the computers were better than doctors.

The authors of *the Fifth Generation* go into more detail about the potentials and qualifications of Dr. Computer. We quote from page 87:

"Many kinds of expertise are unevenly distributed in the world. Medicine is a perfect example. That is one reason the U.S. National Institute of Health has been at the forefront of supporting expert systems research ... If the idea of a machine doctor repels you, consider that not everyone feels that way. Studies in England showed that many humans were much more comfortable with an examination by a computer terminal than with a human physician, whom they perceived as somehow disapproving of them. 'Mechanical' doctors are in fact systems that move methodically through possibilities, making inferences and drawing conclusions. They often outperform the very experts who have programmed them because of their methodical ways; they don't skip or forget things, get tired or rushed, or fall subject to some of our other human failing. They will be on call at the patient's convenience, not just the physician's. And they can bring medicine to places where none now exists."

It appears that because doctors today have become so unemotional and egocentric, that patients of computer doctors prefer their bedside manner to that of human doctors. And, how would a patient go about suing a computer for malpractice?

Christians are instructed to pray for the sick, and we are told in Psalm 103: 2,3. "Bless the Lord, O my soul, and forget not all his benefits; Who forgiveth all thine iniquities; who healeth all thy diseases."

With the advent of the modern doctor with all his laboratory aids and miracle drugs, we have altered our prayers to the intent that God will give our doctors wisdom and direct his hands as he operates.

How are Christians now to pray for a computer?

In the field of medicine the computer is destined to also attain divine-like qualities in human thought.

The Fifth Generation computer has been on the drawing boards since 1978. The American computer industry, which has led the world, has been reticent to bring in the Fifth Generation Age because it has been uncertain what it would do to human society in economics, education, military defense, science, politics and religion. However, Japan has now forced computer scientists in the United States into a decision. They must now produce these new machines, which some contend will not be machines at all, but organic, thinking entities. If the United States computer industry fails to produce the Fifth Generation computer, then Japan will conquer the world market. This amounts to a computer Pearl Harbor.

We quote from page 12 of *The Fifth Generation*: "The Japanese are planning the miracle product. It will come not from their mines, their wells, their fields, or even their seas. It comes instead from their brains. The miracle product is knowledge, and the Japanese are planning to package and sell it the way other nations package and sell energy, food, or manufactured goods. They're going to give the world the next generation — Fifth Generation — of computers, and those machines are going to be intelligent... In October 1981, when Japan first let the world at large know about its plans for the Fifth Generation of computers, the Japanese government announced that over the next decade it planned to spend seed money of $450 million and would eventually involve several hundred top scientists in this project. Their goal is to develop computers for the 1990s and beyond — intelligent computers that will be able to converse with humans in natural language and understand speech and pictures. These will be computers that can learn, associate, make inference, make decisions, and often behave in ways we have always considered the exclusive province of human reason."

The authors of *The Fifth Generation* continue to quote Japanese sources which claim that the new bio-computers will solve the world's unemployment, energy shortages, medical costs, problems that come with old age, industrial inefficiency, food shortages and money crises. It has been estimated by one computer expert that all the memory and data that is in all the present computers in all the world could be stored in a space no bigger than a sugar cube in a Fifth Generation computer.

Major credit card companies and commercials are already preparing for the Fifth Generation Computer age.

Carol Hutchings, who has served in the Southwest Radio Church as supervisor of our own computer department, received a notice in the mail from VISA which reads in part: "You are on the threshold of a new age ... an age in which computers make miracles happen ... I'm inviting you to step over that threshold and accept the credit card for a new age in shopping: With SUPER CARD you get a computer line to the most advanced shopping service in the world ... SUPER CARD is honored at over three million stores ... in more than 150 countries around the world. But what puts your SUPER CARD light years ahead of an ordinary VISA, is an electronic miracle called COMP-U-CARD ... COMP-U-CARD's computer keeps track to the latest near wholesale prices on more than 60,000 brand name items ... you can buy the item and save from 10% to 40% off the manufacturer's suggested list price. Now you can leave 20th century shopping behind."

The advertising letter continues to explain that all shopping can be done by telephone. In addition, the applicant for a SUPER CARD is sent a check for $250 as a bonus, and we quote again: "The Credit Card for 21st Century shopping. The SUPER CARD with COMP-U-CARD is the revolutionary new VISA credit card that lets you shop the way the rest of the world will shop tomorrow —

through the electronic magic of the computer."

Carol did make application for the SUPER CARD, and not only received one in the mail, but also a check for $250.

Nineteen hundred years ago the Apostle John wrote in Revelation 12 that the day would come when all the world would worship the image of the beast that would command all to work, buy and sell through a system of marks and numbers. According to Fifth Generation Computer experts, that day may be less than a decade away.

In considering the prophecy of the Apostle John that a system of buying, selling and working with marks and numbers would be used by a world government to force everyone to worship the Antichrist as god, we refer to an article in *Time* magazine, April 2, 1984 edition, page 65. This article suggests that with scientific advancements made in telephone-computer communications, that before long large department stores and salesclerks will become obsolete, because most buying and selling will be done from the home living room.

On page two of the same edition of *Time*, Mobil Oil Company has an ad simply headed, "1984."

As an example of what the Fifth Generation Computer holds for us, we refer to this ad, "At this point, some three months into the new year, you may be forgiven if you are already sick of reading stories with '1984' in the headlines — stories about how near we are to George Orwell's 'vision' — stories decrying the computer age... While the strides society has made since Orwell's day in electronics, communication, and computerization could theoretically put powerful weapons in the hands of an oppressor, they have in reality put powerful tools in the hands of the average citizen. So we'd like to stand '1984' on its head and examine not the oppressiveness of Big Brother, but the usefulness of Little Computer."

The ad continues to report that in Norway a motorist can drive into a Mobil service station, insert a bank debit card, and fill up his gas tank even though no attendant is on duty.

In Australia a motorist can write the number of a tire or any auto part on a pad, the pad speaks into the telephone and the part is delivered. In Belgium a motorist can put a *franc* bill into the computerized gas terminal and buy gasoline. No attendants are on duty at all.

Mobil is in the process of installing such computerized gas pumps and facilities in 2,400 Mobil stations across the United States.

The ad concludes: "The new computerized system will cut down on business costs — such as operating expenses, fraud losses, and record-keeping — and it saves time and creates more conveniences for the customer. These glimpses from around the world take different forms... But from Japan to Scandanavia, and from New York to Los Angeles, the computer, the customer, and the service station are coming together in new and exciting ways that benefit both business and consumer. And it's happening in 1984."

In every strata of manufacturing, sales, service and even the arts, business analysts are predicting a rosy future in the Fifth Generation Computer Age.

We quote from page 62 of the January 30, 1984

edition of *Business Week*: "When the Japanese rolled out the first models of a new system designed to replace the record played 18 months ago, they hailed these compact disc products as the forerunners of a revolution in the stagnating $11 billion world audio business. Their idea was to rekindle the growth of stereo hi-fi by switching to the digital code of computers to record and play back music."

We are reminded of the prophecy concerning Antichrist in Daniel 8:25, "And through his policy also he shall cause craft to prosper in his hand; and he shall magnify himself in his heart, and by peace shall destroy many: he shall also stand up against the Prince of princes; but he shall be broken without hand."

Governments in all nations are the biggest users of computers and computers are rapidly taking over jobs once performed by bureaucrats.

An article on page 61 of the April 2, 1984 edition of the *U.S. News and World Report* states in part: "Where he goes, Treasury Secretary Donald Regan takes along a portable computer that he uses to keep abreast of a wide range of fast-changing economic data fed from Washington ... At least two Supreme Court Justices now write their formal court opinions on electronic word processors ... In 1983, the government spent some 12 billion dollars — double the amount of five years earlier — to purchase, operate and maintain 18,000 large and medium-sized computers. Not included are hundreds of thousands of small computers ... Under a five-year plan begun last April, the government's computer expenditures will total 28 billion dollars by 1988... Recently the Internal Revenue Service got a green light to proceed with a sweeping modernization program that could have profound effect on American attitudes about paying taxes. This year the IRS began using optical-character recognition equipment to process some 18 million tax returns... The scanners, which can read, number and perform all other processing of the forms at the rate of 10,000 operations per hour, will allow close examinations of far more returns than ever before... Computer matching is rapidly becoming a routine way to ferret out waste and abuse throughout the government ... Computer specialists say that changes in the way the government delivers services are just beginning. They predict savings of billions of dollars as more sophisticated computers take over routine bureaucratic assignments."

The February 10, 1984 edition of the *Washington Post* reported that Giant Food Incorporated and Safeway are in the process of installing computerized Electronic Funds Transfer check-out machines in their supermarkets. However, one banking official observed, "As long as Giant and Safeway offer cash authorization systems, the customer has no incentive to use automated teller machines." In other words, cash and checks will have to go.

On an international basis the computer is merging all nations into a single economic system.

We quote from an article titled "Telecommunications: The Global Battle" on page 126 of the October 24, 1983 edition of *Business Week*: "That world (the world of yesterday) is fast coming apart. Technology is changing so rapidly that equipment formerly enjoying a 30-year life cycle is becoming obsolete almost as fast as it is installed. As quickly as new technology creates new products, customers everywhere want a wider choice of telecommunications services ... The stakes in this new global battle are enormous."

The computer is now making its presence known in outer space. New computer technology and laser breakthroughs have influenced our government to make plans for war in the heavens.

An item in the April 1984 bulletin of *The Research Institute of America* is headed: "A Year Closer To Star Wars Defense — Pentagon And High Tech Planners have Pushed Ahead With President Reagan's Controversial 'Star Wars' Missile Defense System."

On the domestic scene there appears to be no limit to the growing dependence on computers.

An article on page 80 of the science magazine *Discover* for May 1984 reports on growing computerized dating and marriage services.

A news story in the April 1, 1984, edition of the *Norman Transcript* published in Norman, Oklahoma, reports on how computers perfectly match the opposite sexes. The article is titled, "Boy Meets Girl — Can Modern Technology Help Romance Bloom?"

The Fourth Generation Computer Age was made possible by the discovery and/or invention of the silicon computer chip which is made from guartz or sand. However, the silicon chip has no defense against outside power sources. Even lightening will burn a silicon chip to a crisp, and it is theorized that a single 50-megaton air blast over Chicago would knock out every single computer in the United States and Canada. However, the next generation of computers will have biochips, and these will actually repel outside interference and would only be destroyed by a close atomic blast.

We quote from the December 1983 edition of *United Airlines Magazine*: "... if you took all the information in all the computers existing in the world today and used biomolecular technology, it would fit into one sugar cube... one could squeeze about one billion times the amount of circuitry into a biochip as into one of today's conventional silicon computer chips."

According to the article, biochips are made from antibodies that are prevalent in the human body that fight disease germs. These antibodies have only a short life span, but through an induced fusion between them and cancer cells, the result is "a wildly reproducing cancer cell resulting in a unique inheritance: an immortal hybrid cell, or hybridoma, that eternally manufactures antibodies, one after another, each identical."

The Fifth Generation Computer will in effect be a living entity. It will reproduce itself and program itself, and theoretically, one super computer could indeed control the total activities of every human being on planet earth.

The Genetronix Laboratories, of Rockville, Maryland, is a leader in biotechnology development.

We quote from a January 31, 1984, newsletter from Genetronix Laboratories to its stockholders: "... we are seeing increasing awareness of biomolecular electronics in government, industry, universities and the general public ... Recently, the U.S. Information Agency has asked us to help produce a demonstration of biomolecular electronics for the U.S. Pavilion at the 1985 World's Fair in Tsukuba, Japan ... We know 1984 will be an important and exciting year for the company."

The super Fifth Generation Computer proposed in the book *The Enchanted Loom* could be considered to be science fiction if it were not for the fact that its author, Dr. Jastrow, is one of the leading scientists of our time. He is professor of astronomy at Columbia University and Earth Sciences at Dartmouth College.

We begin quoting from page 159 of his book:

"In theory, computers could have been built long ago with gates having many inputs, just like the human brain. However, even a small computer of this kind would need hundreds of billions of separate wires for its gate-to-gate connections. A computer with billions of wires would be impossible to build in practice. The new chips change all that. In these chips there are no wires; the connections are microscopically small. This development ... is a breakthrough in computer evolution, because it makes it possible to build a computer with gates that work like the gates in the human brain. Such computers will come into existence in the 1990s ... They will match the human mind in many respects, and will possess attributes of intelligent life — responsiveness to the world around them, the ability to learn by experience, and quick grasp of new ideas. Will they be living organisms? Most people would say that a computer can never

be a living organism, because it has no feelings or
emotions; it does not eat, or move, or grow ...
Most of these attributes could easily be built into
computers if they were desired ... if its batteries
run low, it can be programmed to move over to an
electrical outlet and plug itself in for a snack ...
Feelings and emotions also can be built into the
computer ... I believe that in a larger cosmic perspective, going beyond the earth and its biological
creatures, the true attributes of intelligent life will
be seen to be those that are shared by man with
the computer— a response to stimuli, absorption of
information around the world, and flexible behavior under changing conditions. The brain that
possesses these attributes may be made of water
and carboncain molecules, and housed in a fragile shell of bone, as our brain is; or it may be made
of metallic silicon, and housed in plastic; but if it
reacts to the world around it, and grows through
experience, it is alive. The era of carbon-chem-
istry life is drawing to a close on the earth and a
new era of silicon-based life — indestructible,
immortal, infinitely expandable— is beginning. By
the turn of the century, ultra-intelligent machines
will be working in partnership with our best minds
on all the serious problems of the day, in an un-
beatable combination of brute reasoning power
and human intuition ... One sees a vision of
mammoth brains that have soaked up the wisdom
of the human race and gone on from there ...
Perhaps man can join forces with the computer to
create a brain that combines the accumulated
wisdom of the human mind with the power of the
machine ... This hybrid intelligence would be the

progenitor of a new race... a bold scientist will be able to tap the contents of his mind and transfer them into the lattices of a computer. Because mind is the essence of being, it can be said that this scientist has entered the computer, and that he now dwells in it. At last the human brain, ensconced in a computer, has been liberated from the weaknesses of the mortal flesh... Man need not wait a thousand years to reach the stars; the stars will come to him."

In Genesis 11:4 Moses recorded that when man first reached for the stars, God said, "... and this they begin to do: and now nothing will be restrained from them, which they have imagined to do."

Of the beast that will take control of the earth before Christ returns, we read, "And he had power to give life unto the image of the beast, that the image of the beast should both speak, and cause that as many as would not worship the image of the beast should be killed. And he causeth all, both small and great, rich and poor, free and bond, to receive a mark in their right hand, or in their foreheads: And that no man might buy or sell, save he that had the mark, or the name of the beast, or the number of his name" (Revelation 13: 15,16).

Will the Antichrist attempt to create a new generation of immortal computerized human beings? It appears that Bible prophecy in this regard is very similar to that envisioned by Dr. Jastrow and others.

In the Iliad, Homer wrote that the god Hephaestus made splendid robots to relieve the gods and goddesses of mundane chores in looking after the human race.

We know from Genesis 6 that much of mythology is based on the true accounts of Satan's effort to subvert God's creation, man, and claim the earth for himself.

Perhaps the Fifth Generation Computer will be another attempt.

In any event, scientists are now working feverishly to fulfill man's demand for bigger, better and more intelligent computers, and God has said, what man has imagined, that he can do.

But there is one thing no computer can do for man.

We quote from the article "Computer Worship" that appears in the May 1984 edition of *Science* magazine: "Massachusetts Institute of Technology computer scientist Joseph Weizenbaum suggests, 'Take the great many people who've dealt with computers now for a long time ... and ask whether they're just as confused and mixed up about the world and their personal relations and so on as anyone else.' "

Only Jesus Christ can give peace of soul and peace of mind. Only Jesus Christ can provide forgiveness of sin and remove the agony of sin that is manifested in a guilty conscience. If you are not now a Christian, receive Jesus Christ as your Saviour and your Lord today.

"For God so loved the world, that he gave his only begotten Son, that whosoever believeth in **him should not perish, but have everlasting life"** (John 3:16).

5

END–TIME WEATHER

As we discussed in our book *War In Heaven*, earth's weather really began acting up in 1977 when the more distant planets began lining up on one side of the sun. The nine planets of our solar system subsequently came into conjunction March 10, 1982.

There is another factor that may have been affecting our weather for several years and seems to be intensifying in 1984. *The Fact Finder*, January 16, 1984, addresses the subject in a pamphlet entitled, "Soviets May Use Tesla Method For 7th Year To Wreck U.S. Weather And Ruin Economy."

Imagine 100-million Americans glued to their television sets watching the superbowl game and not knowing about the biggest game to conquer the world. They have already taken over 27 nations! Score one for our side: We took back Grenada. Big Deal! That's 27 to 1.

Those 100-million Americans have probably never even taken time to learn how the Soviets can modify our weather to cause blizzards, floods and droughts in the United States.

For seven years now, since 1977, many Americans agree that we have suffered "the worst winter weather in U.S. history." Our weather last December was definitely the worst in our history—almost nationwide.

In former years our winter air currents came directly across the warm Pacific giving us a moderate winter. But, starting in 1977, the jet streams in the ionosphere have shifted to hit us from the Arctic regions. This shifts blizzards that would normally fall on Siberia to fall, instead, on the United States. This year our citrus crops in Florida, Louisiana and Texas have already been frozen. This can cause our orange juice to cost much more this year. And shifting blizzards to us can make it possible to grow more crops in Siberia next spring and summer.

Don't laugh until you learn how it can be done!

Russian scientists have for years tried innovative weather-modification techniques. Their rockets and heavy artillery have fired leadiodide crystals into storm clouds to reduce hail. The Russians now admit they are using something else— but they won't say what. The Soviet Union has been conducting mysterious, high-frequency radio experiments that have disrupted some international communications. The Soviets are now experimenting with more sophisticated techniques — for a wireless system of transmitting electricity into the ionosphere for weather-modification.

Their main objective is to push the cold, Arctic air mass that is over Siberia and the Soviet Union over the North Pole to America. This is to increase their agricultural growing season and to greatly reduce ours.

The Russian method of transmitting electric power without the use of wires was known as the "Tesla" process, named after Nicolai Tesla, a scientist who lived from 1856 to 1943. Tesla was an American electrical scientist and inventor, born in Austria-Hungary but immigrated to the United States in 1884. He worked for a while with Edison and became a naturalized American citizen.

A pioneer in high tension electricity, he made discoveries and inventions of great value to the development of radio transmission and in the field of electricity, including this system of transmitting electrical power without wire. Tesla succeeded in lighting 200 electric light bulbs 25 miles away without wires. He was working on experiments in weather-modification when he died in 1943.

The Carter Administration also arranged for the Soviets to have a giant $14-million computer for "weather research." This giant computer, known as Cyber and manufactured by Control Data Corporation of Minneapolis, was far more powerful than any computer available to the Reds at that time.

Early in 1974 the National Severe Storms Forecast Center in Kansas City noted a shift in the jet stream wind patterns. This unexplained change of direction caused an inquiry by the Central Intelligence Agency which in August 1974 prepared a classified working paper entitled, "A Study Of Climatological Research As It Pertains To Intelligence Problems."

The CIA weather experts reported that a climatic change was taking place and that it had caused major economic problems in the world. The study was declassified and released for publication in 1975, but all information pertaining to Soviet weather-modification experiments had been deleted on the recommendation of the state department. The secretary of state at that time was Henry Kissinger.

Time and again, during these last seven years, our Arctic blizzards have been so severe that many of our people have frozen to death in their cars. Transportation has been blocked by air-driven snow that drifted up to 14 feet or more. Time after time airports were closed; schools were closed; factories were closed; and our economy suffered.

Hot summer droughts destroyed crops in some sections while floods in others destroyed people's homes. How much does our government know that they have not told our people for fear of fanning public anger into demanding that our government force the Soviets to stop their war of manipulating our weather?

The earth's ecology which makes life possible on this planet is delicately balanced. According to often quoted scientific sources, the rise or fall of average temperatures three degrees will either bring on an ice age or melt the ice caps causing floods and inundating entire islands and reducing continental land masses. Such metropolitan areas like New York City or Los Angeles could be submerged under several hundred feet of water.

The May 11, 1976, edition of the *St. Paul Dispatch*, reported:

"No nation anywhere in the world, especially in Russia, China, India and the United States, can afford to take lightly the ominous ... century weather forecast covering the entire planet and prepared for the CIA ... It is a calmly chilling and scholarly meteorological study pointing to radical changes in the climate as to cause its authors to warn that ... the consequences in political and economic upheaval and international violence will be 'almost beyond human comprehension.'

"The CIA may have misjudged the oncoming 1973 Yom Kippur war in the Middle East, but it would be perilous to assume that its report is misjudging the oncoming weather that every continent will be experiencing during the rest of the 20th century and during the lifetimes of every human being on this planet ... It's imperative is human survival without such frustration and fear that war becomes inevitable because of massive starvation and death ... Over the vast areas of the earth's land mass, that even now cannot produce enough food to feed all mankind, the signs now accumulating point to these forecasts: There will be destructive droughts where droughts have not been occurring. The climatic changes that have taken place during the past five years can, the experts are convinced, bring consequences such as the following: The Soviet Union ... would lose the lush wheat fields of the entire Kazakhstan. China would experience a major famine ... Droughts would grip India ... resulting in starvation for 150 million people. Canada would lose 50 percent of its productive capacity. Europe's food exports would drop to zero. The United States would be least affected ... but with food shortages stalking the whole world, the U.S. would provide only marginal and selective assistance ... "

The Bible links erratic weather to the last days just prior to the second coming of Christ.

"And there shall be signs in the sun, and in the moon, and in the stars; and upon the earth distress of nations, with perplexity; the sea and the waves roaring; Men's hearts failing them for fear, and for looking after those things which are coming on the earth: for the powers of heaven shall be shaken. And then shall they see the Son of man coming in a cloud with power and great glory. And when these things begin to come to pass, then look up, and lift up your heads; for your redemption draweth nigh" (Luke 21:25-28).

The sea constitutes approximately three-fourths of the earth's surface and ecological forces originating over the oceans control the type of weather prevailing over the land masses.

Evidence that there is a drastic world-change in earth's weather patterns was introduced in an article, which is entitled "El Nino: The World Turns Topsy-Turvy."

"When it began, the sea change was not recognized for what it was. Northwest of this port town, the isolated reach of the eastern Pacific Ocean along the Equator remained misleadingly benign. The few who sailed near at the time remember an eerie, beautiful stillness — a flat sea of glassy waters and little wind . . . But the temperature of the sea surface during May 1982 had risen slightly, less than one degree Fahrenheit. Reports of the subtle warming, measured by weather satellites and drifting buoys deployed by the United States' National Oceanographic and Atmospheric Administration, flowed that month into the suburban Camp Springs, Maryland, office of Gene Rasmusson, chief of the diagnostics branch of Climate Analysis Center. Rasmusson thought the readings odd, particularly because the Southern Hemisphere was entering its winter season, but he figured the satellite data probably was faulty . . . A few eyebrows were raised. Then the scientists went on to other business. 'In retrospect, we should have been able to figure what was happening,' Oregon State University oceanographer William Quinn said a year later. 'The signs were there.' "

What was happening was the beginning of a natural catastrophe unequated in this century, associated with a warm ocean current called *El Nino*. In the past year, disrupted weather patterns have wreaked havoc across three-fourths of the globe causing more than 800 deaths and $8 billion in damage.

Nevertheless, the Scriptures indicate quite plainly that the reason for the Tribulation, when even nature will be reversed and serve as a messenger of judgment from God, will be to bring the human race to an acknowledgment that there is a Creator who made the universe and to whom man is accountable for his works in this life.

Even after three and one-half years of judgments when one-third of the world's population will be killed, the nations will still refuse to recognize God as the all-powerful Creator.

We read in Revelation 9:20,21:

"And the rest of the men which were not killed by these plagues yet repented not of the works of their hands ... Neither repented they of their murders, nor of their sorceries, nor of their fornication nor of their thefts."

According to a scientific survey published in the August 1, 1983, edition of *U.S. News And World Report*, weather changes relate to man in the following ways:

1. Changes in air pressure and humidity have a profound effect on arthritis, heart disorders, and sinus problems. More people die from heart attacks in periods of extreme heat or extreme cold.

2. Adverse weather is related to mental illness by putting added stress on people. Rainy weather contributes to gloominess and depression. More people are admitted to mental hospitals on days when the humidity is high than any others and more people commit suicide on days when the humidity is high than on other days.

3. Wind linked with conditions of humidity also has a definite psychological effect. We quote from page 52 of the article referred to in *U.S. News And*

World Report:

"A warm, dry wind — sometimes called the foehn —has been linked in a number of countries, including the U.S., Switzerland and Israel, with an increase in psychiatric disorders and mental-hospital admissions. People are found to have difficulty solving problems. Their reaction is slowed down and they are more irritable."

4. During hot and humid days there are more assaults with associated rapes, murders and riots than on temperate, cool or cold days.

5. Excessive hot or cold weather renders the human anatomy more susceptible to disease germs than at other times. Plagues and epidemics like cholera and pneumonia occur in times of extreme heat or cold.

According to experts, our weather is changing, even becoming chaotic. Established ocean currents are even flowing in the opposite directions. Areas that normally receive six inches of rain a year got over twelve feet of rain this past year. Other areas in the world that normally receive 30 inches to 60 inches a year had practically no rain at all.

According to scientists who are studying these climatic global patterns, these changes are more than the temperamental behavior tantrums of mother nature. We believe this is just another way **God is witnessing to the world to prepare for the** return of His Son from Heaven, the Lord Jesus Christ, who will come with the angels of Heaven to judge those who know not God and who obey not the Gospel.

An example of the catastrophic weather in 1982 is that in Peru and Bolivia there was a drought resulting in damages of $240 million, while in Brazil, Argentina and Paraquay there was flooding that killed 170 people, 600,000 people lost their homes, and the resulting damages amounted to $3 billion.

This example is typical of drastic weather changes around the entire globe.

We quote from page 19 of the *Los Angeles Times:*

"In desert areas of Peru, Ecuador and Bolivia, where the climate is normally so arid that roofs are not built watertight, 12 feet of rain had fallen, compared to a norm of 4 to 5 inches. Meanwhile, in agricultural regions of north Bolivia and south Peru, there had been no rain in eight months... roads, including the Pan American Highway, ended in lakes several miles long. Some 40,000 adobe homes had melted... The Galapagos saw more rain in one six-week period than it normally sees in six years... U.S. officials began to fear that the disruption caused by the natural catastrophes was serious enough to threaten the stability of the Andean democracies of Peru, Ecuador and Bolivia... On the other side of the Pacific, Australia had endured property and crop damage of $1.2 billion ... Cattle, sheep and goats died by the thousands ... Zimbabwe ... faced the need to relocate 1 million head of cattle. Micronesia was running out of drinking water and facing serious public health problems, including an outbreak of infectious hepatitis... Between January and June, Ponape and Yap, which usually get 180 and 110 inches of rain respectively, received just 7 and 5.5 inches... Indonesia endured 340 deaths and $650 million in crop damage..."

This story continues to list country after country that suffered storm, drought or flood damage in 1983, with the pattern indicating a total reversal of established weather patterns.

Again, we note that Bible prophecy for the last days indicates droughts, floods, overflowing rains, storms with hailstones so huge they will kill men and beast.

The prophet Joel gave the following description:

"Alas for the day? for the day of the Lord is at hand, and as a destruction from the Almighty shall it come... The seed is rotten under their clods, the garners are laid desolate, the barns are broken down; for the corn is withered. How do the beast groan... because they have no pasture; yea, the flocks of sheep are made desolate... The beast of the field cry also unto thee: for the rivers of water are dried up, and the fire hath devoured the pastures of the wilderness" (Joel 1:1, 17, 18, 20).

There are doubtless other factors involved besides weather-war. There are storms on the sun, continued alignment of the planets through 1985 and pollution of our ionisphere.

Let's again consider possible side-effects of continuing Russian experiments in the electrical force-field above our planet.

It has been estimated that between the Earth's surface and the top of the atmosphere there is an electric potential of around two billion volts. But the availability of this energy could be at best a

mixed blessing as conjecture has already con-
nected some frightening incidents internationally
with attempts to tap earth-electricity.

In October 1976 the world's radio and radar
systems went haywire with an entirely new kind of
interference. The source was pinpointed at Riga,
a small Russian town 1,000 kilometers west of
Moscow. In answer to protests Russia apologized,
explaining that they had just been doing a few
frequency experiments. Two months later the interference occured again, but this time it was much
worse. Huge standing waves, 1,500 kilometers
long were reported all over the world.

At the same time it was reported that in Russia a
nationwide search was going on for anyone who
had ever known or met Tesla.

Early in 1977 meteorologists reported a strange
"blocking effect" extending down the west coast
of America and a similar one on the east coast and
along the Russo-Polish border up to Finland.
These blocks were stopping the normal circulation
of, and seemed to be associated with, very large
standing waves of electro-magnetic energy.

Whether these "blocking effects" were from the
same source in Russia as the 1976 incidents is
not known. But while they lasted, world weather
was drastically affected.

Snow fell in Miami and floods swept Europe.

It was quite feasible, however, that the bizarre
weather was, in fact, merely a side-effect of what-
ever experiments were being carried out at Riga
and some experts have explained the phenomena
as the climate "hitting back."

To quote a Canadian report:

"Either they (the Russians) have discovered some revolutionary new technique or we are the victims of some new experiment which has gone wrong and drastically upset the weather balance."

It does seem likely that any attempt to draw on earth-electricity on a large scale could lead to unpredictable repercussions in weather for it is, after all, a way of tampering with the atmosphere. To lay all the blame at the doorstep of the Russians, however, would be grossly unfair. It seems more likely that many nations are now working on tapping earth-electricity, and if so, we can expect more incidents of freak weather and strange patterns of interference in radio and navigation signals.

While some blame Russia for the frightening change in the weather, others believe that the sun is the culprit. That the sun affects the weather on earth is obvious.

If the heat from the sun were just a few degrees hotter, life as we know it would not be possible. Or, if the heat received from the sun was much less, the earth would be a ball of ice. It is the sun that heats the oceans and land mass causing water evaporation that produces rain and wind currents which in turn bring rain from the sea over the land.

Another weather-changing factor from the sun is solar flares.

Our sun is a huge atomic reactor which works on the fusion rather than the fission principle. God designed it for the job it was to do and it has been fulfilling this task since the fourth day of creation.

Jesus prophesied about the sun:

"Immediately after the tribulation of those days

shall the sun be darkened, and the moon shall not give her light, and the stars shall fall from heaven, and the powers of the heavens shall be shaken:" (Matthew 24:29).

During the coming Great Tribulation, the Apostle John saw the moon becoming as blood and the sun so hot it scorched men on the earth and burned all the grass (Rev. 6:12; 16:8,9).

Put these prophecies together and they accurately describe a nova of our sun during the Great Tribulation. Increased solar flares and a reduction in the sun's energy production could indicate that this could be nearer than we may believe. In any event, some weather experts blame these sun spots for the unpredictable weather for the past year.

An article from the *Washington Post* dated April 20, 1982, had this to say about the sun's relation to weather:

"A U.S. satellite has compiled data indicating an almost steady drop in the sun's energy. That could have been a cause of this year's harsh winter . . . the sun lost as much as one-twentieth of 1 percent of its energy through all of 1980 . . . The foremost proponent that the 'solar constant,' as it has long been called, is an inconstant number, is Dr. John A. Eddy of the High Altitude Observatory in Boulder, Colorado. Their telescopes have recorded images of what appears to be a shrinking sun. Boulder has found that the sun may have been losing as much as a meter and a half of its diameter every hour along the equator and may have been shrinking by as much as one-tenth of 1 percent every

100 years for the last four centuries."

According to this article, in the previous 18 months there has been a continuing decline in the sun's energy output, and a decline in the sun's heat of one-half of one-percent caused the so-called "Little Ice Age" of the 17th century.

An article in the April 1982 edition of *Science Magazine* tentatively suggested:

"The sun's energy comes from the thermo-nuclear reactions... There is, however, no certainty that the rate of energy release will remain constant; any variations would be of considerable scientific interest and profoundly important for man's well-being."

Another theory concerning the changing weather has been the increase in the number of volcanoes in the past few years, resulting in larger amounts of volcanic ash in the atmosphere. In 1974, two astronomers, John R. Gribbin and Stephen H. Plagemann, predicted that at the next conjunction of the planets, which occurred in the winter of 1982, that there would be earthquakes all over the earth, catastrophic weather, and many other environmental disasters. The theory was that as the sun reached its solar-flare apex, the alignment of the planets would exert added influence resulting in increased sunspot activity.

According to the two astronomers in a later edition of their book, *The Jupiter Effect*, they missed the maximum solar activity period of the sun by two years. However, they claim that the alignment of the planets, even in the preceding two years when lesser conjunctions occurred, was responsible for the eruption of Mt. St. Helens and other volcanic eruptions around the world. They also point to increased earthquake activity in the 1980-1982 period.

In the concluding paragraph of the revised edition of *The Jupiter Effect*, the authors state:

"The next change of gear in the sun's rhythms, the next minimum of solar activity, is due in about five years' time, perhaps in 1986 or 1987, and the next solar maximum is due in 1991. The saga is far from being over."

Concerning erupting volcanoes, it appears that the ring of fire around the earth is already burning as fiery prelude to Armageddon.

From the *Star* publication, September 20, 1983, comes this startling headline: "33 Volcano Time-Bombs Ticking In Countdown To Catastrophe."

Under the heading "Fire & Brimstone," *Time* Magazine, April 9, 1984, gives a description of a double eruption in Hawaii, the first time since 1868:

"When the world's largest active volcano erupted for the first time in nine years, it did so with spectacular fury. Fountains of fiery lava shot 400 feet into the air from the 1½-mile-wide crater at the summit of Mauna Loa (13,677 ft). The lava spilled down blackened mountain slopes in thick rivers of gleaming marigold fire, looking demonically magical; an apprentice sorcerer's wish for gold gone awry. At week's end the menacing wall had oozed to within four miles of Hawaii's second-largest city, Hilo, (population 35,000).

"As Mauna Loa's flow started to slow, its famous and recently active neighbor, Kilauea, 20 miles away, began a new eruption of its own: it is the first

time the two volcanoes have spurted simultane-
ously since 1868. There were, in addition, apocalyptic rumblings on the mainland, where Washington State's Mount St. Helens was once more
sputtering smoke and ash."

It does seem that since 1977 our weather has
been very erratic and the weather pattern since
that time bodes nothing good for mankind. We
note again that disastrous weather in 1983 affected three-fourths of the earth resulting in 800
deaths and property damages totaling $8 billion.

We can expect the tempo of castastrophe to accelerate in 1984.

Earthquakes have steadily increased in number and intensity since the beginning of this century.

The authors of *The Jupiter Effect* — Gribben
and Plagemann — predict a massive earthquake
in California for this decade.

According to the *New York City Daily News*,
October 9, 1983, experts warned that the midwest is due for a massive earthquake and said
residents, lulled by years of stable ground, are
woefully unprepared.

Nature will strike out at the sinfulness of man
and weather. War will not be the least of God's
arsenal that will literally shake the heavens and
the earth (Hebrews 12:25-29).

6

SECULAR HUMANISM — DEVIL'S DOCTRINE

Jesus said there would one day come a generation in which a myriad of specific signs would point to the imminence of His return. As the end of the age approaches, more and more signs appear.

Humanism is a word we are hearing often.

What is Humanism? Webster's New Collegiate Dictionary defines Humanism as: "A doctrine, attitude, or way of life centered on human interests or values; esp: a philosophy that asserts the dignity and worth of man and his capacity for self-realization through reason and that often rejects supernaturalism."

We read in Revelation 3:14-18, 20:

"And unto the angel of the church of the Laodiceans write; These things said the Amen, the faithful and true witness, the beginning of the creation of God; I know thy works, that thou art neither cold nor hot; I would thou wert either cold or hot. So then because thou art lukewarm, and neither cold nor hot, I will spue thee out of my mouth. Because thou sayest, I am rich, and increased with goods, and have need of nothing; and knowest not that thou art wretched, and miserable, and poor, and blind, and naked: I counsel thee to buy of me gold tried in the fire, that thou mayest be rich; and white raiment, that thou mayest be clothed, and that the shame of thy nakedness do not appear; and anoint thine eyes with eyesalve, that thou mayest see... Behold, I stand at the door, and knock: if any man hear my voice, and open the door, I will come in to him, and will sup with him, and he with me."

According to Bible scholars, we are currently living in the Laodicean church period.

The word Laodicea comes from two Greek words, *laos* and *dike*. These two words happen to be predominant in world circles today. Laos means "people" or "human," and *dike* means "rights" thus "human rights."

This is precisely the condition prevailing in the world today. There is a one-world religious system that is invading every stratum of society. It is described by the Apostle John as being lukewarm, not hot or cold, a condition that nauseates our holy God.

We are part of this generation that looks at itself as being rich and having need of nothing, while blinding ourselves to our real moral and spiritual state.

One writer described this generation as "wretched though they may dance and sing; pitiable, though lauded by princes, premiers, and peers; blind though the physical optics are sound; and naked, though robed in splendour."

What a terrible self-deception!

Festus wrote: "The first and worst of all frauds is to cheat one's self. All sin is easy after that."

Yet we see the patience and long-suffering of our loving Lord Jesus toward the Laodicean church, the poorest of all the churches. In the church period, there is nothing to be commended. The Lord Jesus Christ Himself is outside the church! He is grieved and dishonored, yet He continues to love and extend His grace to this ego-centric generation. The devil's lie that began in the garden, "ye shall be as gods" (Genesis 3:5), continues to work in the hearts of men to this day.

WHAT DO HUMANISTS BELIEVE?

Very few Americans know about this new religion taking over our land. It is not singled out by the media as are the other false cults, such as the "moonies." It is because the media, for the most part, are members of this religion.

The goals of the Humanists are very clear and simple: to bring about the establishment of a one-world government and an atheistic one-world church. It will be a "new world order" totally controlled by the state.

What do the Humanists believe? Humanism:

1. Denies the deity of God, the inspiration of the Bible, and the deity of the Lord Jesus.

2. Denies the existence of the soul, life after death, salvation, Heaven, and damnation in Hell.

3. Denies the biblical account of creation.

4. Believes there are no absolutes — no right, no wrong — that moral values are self-determined and situational. Do your own thing "as long as it does not harm anyone else."

5. Believes in removal of distinctive roles of male and female.

6. Believes in sexual freedom between consenting individuals, regardless of age, including pre-marital sex, homosexuality, lesbianism and incest.

7. Believes in the right to abortion, euthanasia (mercy killing) and suicide.

8. Believes in equal distribution of America's wealth to reduce poverty and bring equality.

9. Believes in control of the environment, control of energy and its limitation.

10. Believes in removal of American patriotism and the free-enterprise system, disarmament and the creation of a socialistic one-world government.

These points are enumerated in *The Humanist Manifestos I* and *II,* Prometheus Books, Buffalo, New York, and the Aspen Institute for Humanistic Studies, according to the *Freemen Digest*, Provo, Utah.

The implications of this humanistic philosophy in the political and social facets of life can be clearly seen in the totalitarian regimes of history. This philosophy justifies the humanist's support of genocide — the systematic killing or termination of people. This is evidenced by practices such as abortion and euthanasia — the proposal of killing millions of our elderly, terminally ill and crippled. Their ultimate goal, as was Hitler's, is to build a master-race by conducting human breeding experiments. Humanists believe in the MECHANISTIC view of man, as opposed to the Bible's divinely determined purpose for man.

B.F. Skinner, Harvard professor and signer of *The Humanist Manifesto II* advocates the abolition of man as an individual.

He says, "His (man's) abolition has long been overdue. Autonomous man IS A DEVICE used to explain what we cannot explain in any other way. To man we readily say good riddance."

Skinner proposes that man be placed in a highly manipulative and regulated environment in order to control him.

This philosophy is accountable for the great bureaucracy that continues to blind us and take away our freedom. The devil's humanistic philosophy says that man is no more than a machine, "junk" that can be discarded when it is deemed undesirable.

Professor Harvey Cox of Harvard Divinity School stated that Humanism "is a dangerous ideological system because it seeks to impose its ideology through the organs of the State."

These impositions are clearly spelled out in the *Humanist Manifestos I* and *II.*

"Manifesto II" written some forty years later, states in its preface:

"As in 1933, humanists still believe that traditional theism, ESPECIALLY FAITH IN THE PRAYER-HEARING GOD, ASSUMED TO LOVE AND CARE FOR PERSONS, TO HEAR AND UNDERSTAND THEIR PRAYERS, AND TO BE ABLE TO DO SOMETHING ABOUT THEM, IS AN UNPROVED AND OUTMODED FAITH. SALVATIONISM, BASED ON MERE AFFIRMATION, STILL APPEARS AS HARMFUL, DIVERTING PEOPLE WITH FALSE HOPES OF HEAVEN HEREAFTER. Reasonable minds look to other means for survival. Traditional moral codes and new irrational cults both fail to meet the pressing needs of today and tomorrow. False 'theologies of hope' and messianic ideologies, substituting new dogmas for old, cannot cope with existing world realities. They separate rather than unite people. Humanism is an ethical process through which we all can move, above and beyond the divisive particulars, heroic personalities, dogmatic creeds, and ritual customs of past religions or their mere negation. As non-theists (commonly known as atheists), we begin with humans, not God, nature not deity ... No deity (God) will save us; we must save ourselves." (Emphasis added).

Even in the face of such blatant unbelief, the

Lord Jesus is still knocking at the heart's door of such people, offering them the forgiveness of sins and personal salvation.

Humanists have even changed the significance of our holidays to eliminate God completely from these celebrations and promote their own ideals.

Present-day humanists regard Christmas, which has already become secularized to a large extent in the United States, as a folk day symbolizing the joy of existence, the feeling of human brotherhood and the ideal of democratic sharing.

Many humanists prefer to stress New Year's Day rather than Christmas. Easter is humanistically utilized to celebrate the "rebirth" of the vital forces of nature and renewal of man's own energies. Even humanist weddings and funeral services, prepared by ethical culture and humanist groups, are already in use.

The confusion of Laodicean theology is expressed in humanism's refusal to believe in miracles, resurrection of the body and in a life after death. God's part in nature or history is excluded, and He becomes "useless" and is viewed as a "dead God." Such thought is the basis of today's humanist religion.

Humanism strongly believes in the inevitability of progress; this is also called social evolution. This idea proposes that nature is moving inevitably to higher and higher forms of life. However, this optimistic view of progress has been rebutted by the history of human behavior in the last forty years.

HUMANISM IN GOVERNMENT
— ITS GOALS

Humanism in government is more deadly than cancer because the government is being used as an agent to minister its philosophy. This ideology has permeated every office of our government.

Historian and philosopher Os Guiness stated:

"As Secular Humanism takes a more pessimistic outlook toward man's progress, humanists look more to the state to assume a guiding hand in shaping man's future. In recent years the state has heeded the humanist call and taken on a more humanistic character. In this respect, education is viewed by Secular Humanism as the fulfillment of the state's role as a saving institution. Because man is either not progressing as rapidly as the Secular Humanist would desire, or because man does not seem to be progressing in the evolutionary sense, many Secular Humanists have opted for FORCED PROGRESS and manipulative environment control. TOTALITARIANISM, therefore, could very well be the end result of Secular Humanism."

This is exactly what the Bible tells us is going to take place. It is happening right before our very eyes and we are even paying for its implementation with our tax money.

HUMANISM — A RELIGION
IN OUR SCHOOLS

Humanists themselves refer to Humanism as a "faith" and a "religion."

The U.S. Supreme Court in 1961 declared Humanism to be a religion (the Torcaso Decision) removing all doubt.

Even though Humanism is now a religion, it is different from the traditional denominations. It does not have special church buildings or Sunday worship services. However, it does have its own "Sunday schools" and its own "Sunday school superintendent." Our public schools are being used to teach the philosophy of Humanism, even though the United States Constitution requires the separation of church and state.

Bible believers are not only paying salaries and expenses of this new religion, but we are also paying the salary of its new "Sunday school superintendent," according to Judge Shirley Hufstedler, first secretary of the newly established Department of Education.

Judge Hufstedler has served as a trustee of the Aspen Institute for Humanistic Studies, which is a major force of the Humanistic movement.

According to Joseph E. Slater, president of the Aspen Institute: " ... The goals of the Aspen Institute vary from ... vital social issues ... to proposals for NEW EDUCATIONAL CURRICULA and innovative programs in the mass media."

Proposals are being carried out by their agents in government, even to the establishing of entire new cabinet departments.

There are many well-meaning Christians who do not understand how these Humanistic beliefs are being implanted in the minds of our children.

The teaching technique known as "Values Clarification," developed by Pavlov under Lenin and Stalin, is being used in our public schools. This

teaches children to ignore their parents' teachings and religious beliefs. They are taught to
create their own personal values, and that there
are NO ABSOLUTES: NO RIGHT, NO WRONG.

This is how the communists train animals.

America's children are being trained to forsake
the influence of their parents and more import-
antly, "freed" from God's standard of right and
wrong, the Bible.

The results are in complete harmony with the
Apostle Paul's declaration of "perilous times" in
the last days, of children being "disobedient to
parents, (and) unholy" (II Timothy 3:1-5).

THE CHURCH OF THE LAODICEANS

Satan's attack against God's people began in
the Garden of Eden and continues unto this day. It
had its beginning when the devil lied. "Yea, hath
God said . . . Ye shall not surely die: For God doth
know that in the day ye eat thereof, then your eyes
shall be opened, and ye shall be as gods, knowing
(or determining for yourself) good and evil"
(Genesis 3:1,4,5).

The devil deceived Adam and Eve into thinking
God was keeping something from them. He suggested that they must be their own rulers,
choosing, knowing, and determining for themselves what is good and evil.

Without the traditional theistic absolutes revealed by God, man must produce a set of ar-
bitrary absolutes by which he can only "hope" to
arrive at an orderly society.

One Humanist has noted: "Materialistic philosophy relieves one of responsibility to anyone,

including the supernatural. Atoms have no morals, thus, if they are our progenitors, man is amoral."

The Bible warns us in Rev. 12:2, "... Woe to the inhabiters of the earth and of the sea! For the devil is come down unto you, having great wrath, because he knoweth that he hath but a short time."

The devil has planted his agents in the Church just as the Bible tells us tares creep up among good wheat. The "false wheat" is doubly dangerous for it pretends to be good as it destroys.

Christianity has suffered more from ungodly professors, false teachers and hypocrites than from the open enemies of the Cross. There are many false teachers disguised as ministers of the Gospel.

The Lavrentia Beria Russian Textbook on Psycho-politics makes the following statement:

"We had to destroy, after many, many years of arduous work, the Church, so we must destroy all faiths in nations marked for conquest... We have battled in America since the century's turn to bring to nothing any and all Christian influences and we are succeeding."

As you can see, there is a very carefully planned conspiracy to destroy the Church. But the Lord Jesus said of the Church to Peter in Matt. 16:18, "... the gates of hell shall not prevail against it."

Part of this conspiracy lies in the World Council of Churches.

Humanism in the Church today can be clearly seen in the efforts of the World Council of Churches (WCC), also known as "the ecumenical movement." They have restored to the Greek word *oikumene* its original secular meaning, "all the inhabitants of the earth."

Many well-meaning Christians who belong to churches that are a part of the WCC are being deceived into thinking that this movement is merely a movement to unite Christendom. They are totally unaware of the un-Christian nature of this Laodicean philosophy and its efforts to destroy Christianity.

A report of the WCC's 1968 Uppsala Assembly says:

"We recognize the importance of cooperating at every level with the Roman Catholic church, with other non-member churches, WITH NON-CHURCH ORGANIZATIONS, ADHERENTS OF OTHER RELIGIONS, MEN OF NO RELIGION, INDEED WITH MEN OF GOODWILL EVERY-WHERE." (Emphasis added).

The word "ecumenical" refers not merely to all Christians, but to men of all religions and those with no religion at all.

This has enabled the WCC to break free from the constraints of a specific Christian identity and advance into a "no man's land" where all ideologies and cultures are equal. The WCC's ecumenical goal is not to unite the Christians — it is to unite all of mankind.

The following paragraphs are quoted from a book by Homer Duncan entitled, *Secular Humanism — The Most Dangerous Religion In America.*

"Today, within the bounds of the Church, we are witnessing a satanic word of deception and substitution that is intended to deceive even the very elect. This giant hoax is the substitution of Humanism for Christianity.

"The welfare of man is a worthy objective. But when that welfare becomes an end in itself, with no reference to man's eternal soul, it is high time for Christians to take a look.

"Humanism's concern is for material values, but Christianity places spiritual values above all else.

"Humanism is concerned with now, with time and all that occurs in the present. Christianity's eyes are set on eternity, on the city made without hands, eternal in the heavens.

"For the humanist, the 'gospel' had to do with man's reconciliation to man; but Christianity's Gospel puts man's reconciliation to God through Jesus Christ above all else.

"The humanist sees 'sin' as primarily man's maladjustment to man; for the Christian, sin is disobedience to God's revealed will.

"Humanism is concerned about man's physical, environmental and material welfare, but not about his soul. Christianity recognizes that only as man is reconciled to God can he be properly adjusted to the conditions of everyday life, and that by the presence and grace of God, situations that otherwise would be unbearable, are often means to draw him closer to God.

"Humanism is willing to make use of any secular power or means to accomplish its ends. Christianity depends on the presence and power of the Holy Spirit for its effectiveness.

"Christians need to recognize the solemn fact that humanism is not an ally in making the world a better place in which to live. It is a deadly enemy for it is a religion without God and without hope in this world or the next.

"The danger lies in the confusion of the objectives of Humanism and Christianity, a confusion rooted in totally divergent concepts of God and man."

HUMANISM AND PUBLIC EDUCATION

Christian leaders have long realized that we are engaged in a gigantic battle for the minds and souls of men. With the rise of Secular Humanism we must realize that we are struggling for the minds of boys and girls and the youth of our nation. This battle is being fought in our public schools and, unknown to most Americans, the humanists have been winning the battle so far in the Twentieth Century.

The false evolutionary hypothesis, which has been widely accepted as a scientific fact, has all but destroyed the basis for education as it existed at the beginning of the century.

It is quite likely that Professor John Dewey of Columbia University had more to do with the molding of educational thought in the early part of the Twentieth Century than any other man.

Dewey's biographer said of him:

"The starting point of his system of thought was biological: he sees man as an organism in an environment, remaking as well as made. Things are to be understood through their origins and functions, without the intrusion of supernatural considerations."

In the early 1920s, spiritually minded educators could see the handwriting on the wall and realized that humanism was on the verge of making a tremendous onslaught on the culture through the public educational system. Now both Christians and Humanists recognize the great impact that evolutionary Humanism has made on traditional theism through the public education system.

Dr. Francis Schaeffer said:

"Everywhere I go I find behaviorists completely committed to (Skinner's) views. Man is accepted as a machine, and he is treated as a machine. Such professionals are there by the hundreds, some of them with understanding, some of them with power, some of them only in little places. In some places they control the educational process down into the earliest days of school."

How have the Humanists been able to gain control of our educational system?

There are several answers to this question.

First, they do it by educating the educators. Students who themselves later will be the teachers are thoroughly indoctrinated in evolutionary Humanism.

Secondly, they do it by controlling the textbooks that are used in the primary schools through the universities.

One of the founders of the older publishing houses is reported to have said, "Let me publish the textbooks of nations and I care not who writes its songs or makes it laws."

Alexander J. Bourke, Jr. states "... textbooks both mirror and create our values."

For those who are interested in making a study of the textbook situation in our schools we strongly recommend *Textbooks On Trial* by James C.

Hefley.

In her paper "The Religion Of Humanism In Public Schools," Barbara Morris writes:

"I often think about the religion of Humanism being promoted in public schools and without fail, I find myself asking, where, oh where are the Christians? Why do those who claim to be true followers of Christ permit this hoax to go unchallenged? Every Christian and every Christian Church should be actively exposing and working to remove this Godless religion from our public schools. One woman's efforts resulted in a ban on prayer and Bible reading. How is it that the people of a nation that claims to be predominantly Christian cannot rout the religion of Humanism from their schools?"

Barbara Morris also raises the question:

"How are the principles of Humanism as outlined in the second Humanist Manifesto applied in public education?"

She answers:

"Very simply. Every course in the curriculum can serve as a vehicle to promote Humanist beliefs... history, math, literature, languages, social studies, sex education, environmental education, home economics ... everything. Over the years during the steady influx of Humanist influence in the schools via the use of Humanist-oriented textbooks and teachers the order of society and God-given human rights are in no way protected. Without any standards of right and wrong, the all-powerful state will continue setting its own standards. The Founding Fathers understood that the only ground on which to base resistance against imposed order was upon Divine Providence, and that freedom is found in the CREATOR, not in man-made documents.

"As Alexander Hamilton proclaimed, 'The sacred rights of mankind are not to be rummaged for among old parchments or musty records. They are written, as with a sunbeam, in the whole volume of human nature, by the hand of the Divinity itself, and can never be erased or obscured by mortal power.' "

Yes, there is a war on, and like it or not, you are in it. The only question is this: On whose side do you stand — with the Lord, or with the great Laodicean Generation? Will you say with Joshua, ". . . As for me and my house, we will serve the Lord" (Joshua 24:15)?

We, too, urge you to hold fast to Christ, and to stand firm against the world's flood of false religion and self-directed philosophy. Salvation is from God, not man, and only in service to God can we truly serve others.

7

SPACE
MAN'S LAST FRONTIER

Man, the pristine rebel, is looking more and more heavenward. He dreams of myriad worlds to conquer, explore and colonize. Scientists talk in technological terms of permanent space stations, space cities and manned rocket trips to other planets in our solar system as early as 1991.

Man is becoming more daring and adventuresome as he dangles outside the safety of his shuttle without his life line or spatial umbilical cord.

Quoting an article from *Discover* Magazine, April 1984, on page 14, entitled "In The Armchair Of The Gods."

"Sunlight, creeping around the blue limb of the earth 175 miles below, began to wash over the hull of the space shuttle Challenger as Bruce

McCandless, in the shadows of the cargo bay, asked permission to abandon ship. 'I'm going to head on out of the bay,' he crackled, 'with your permission.' With his left hand he pulled up on a small handle on the armrest of his square white backpack, which looked for all the world like a bulky, legless chair. A burst of compressed nitrogen gas shot from tiny thrusters, and McCandless rose head first out of the shuttle, his dangling legs silhouetted against the bright cloud tops of the earth. As he cleared the bay, the astronaut twisted another knob on his right armrest and flipped to face the shuttle. Then he backed cautiously off into the void, dwarfed by the blackness around him as he receded. 'This is neat,' he reported. Then looking down, he exclaimed, 'Looks like Florida — it is Florida! It's the Cape!' Sailing over the clouds at 17,000 miles per hour, McCandless had become a human spaceship.

"As Stewart watched, McCandless climbed into his backpack and checked out the controls while it was mounted in a wall rack in the cargo bay. Then he floated away from the wall and began flying around the bay. Meanwhile, Stewart practiced manipulating tools in zero gravity at work stations designed to resemble satellites that astronauts hope to repair in space some day.

"McCandless's historic first voyage took him 150 feet away from the mother ship and lasted about twelve minutes. Scudding alone and tiny over the cloud tops far below, he looked like nothing so much as a Zeus blown by some cosmic gust from his Mount Olympus perch, throne and all.

"After moving as far as 320 feet from the shuttle, he approached again and asked, 'Are you going to want me to wash the windows or anything while I'm out here?' His kind offer refused, it was Stewart's turn to take the backpack.

"The image of that moment will linger as long as humans fly and dream of challenging the stars. Powered by Buck Rogers backpacks, known as manned maneuvering units (MMUs), McCandless and fellow astronaut Robert Stewart became the first human beings to venture from their space-craft without a lifeline. Their untethered flights, their ability to navigate freely, away from the shuttle, cleared the way for a host of new activi-ties in space. Among them: the first space rescue — the scheduled capture and repair in April of the disabled Solar Max astronomical satellite and the assembly of an American space station by the early 1990s. Said McCandless, 'We've opened a new frontier.'

"For much of Challenger's eight-day flight in February, it hardly seemed that way. Two $75 million communications satellites were lost in space; the shuttle toilet clogged again; and on its long-awaited, first-ever landing at the Kennedy Space Center in Florida, the shuttle smacked into a bird."

Right out of Buck Rogers and Flash Gordon, man is exercising his God-like powers with great enthusiasm and to global applause.

But before man builds Babel, God says, you are a trespasser, I will bring you down; I will send you back.

Psalm 115:16 declares: "The heaven, even the heavens, are the Lord's: but the earth hath he given to the children of men."

Obviously man is not well suited for outer space. Zero gravity can make him dizzy and he has to take his oxygen with him wherever he goes. Man is a frail creature at best and the Bible states that in his present physical body he has no inheritance in the heavens.

"Now this I say, brethren, that flesh and blood cannot inherit the kingdom of God; neither doth corruption inherit incorruption" (I Corinthians 15:50).

However, man truly demonstrated his ingenuity in repairing the satellite Solar Max in the recent space shuttle.

Quoting *Time* Magazine, April 9, 1984, page 106, an article entitled, "Tinkering With Solar Max:"

"Every eleven years the sun's outer layers erupt in a blaze of turbulent magnetic storms, characterized by an increase in sunspots and fiery explosions known as solar flares. In February 1980, on the eve of one such outburst, NASA launched an instrument-packed scientific satellite called the Solar Maximum Mission. Nicknamed Solar Max, the spacecraft was to photograph and monitor the sun's activity, which even at a distance of 93 million miles can disrupt global communications and power transmissions, influence weather and endanger space voyagers.

"After ten months in orbit, however, Solar Max blew three critical fuses. The failure impaired its ability to keep properly turned toward the sun, left it wobbling like a top, and triggered breakdowns in its battery of instruments. The $325 million Solar Max program seemed moribund.

"For the first time, the deltawinged spacecraft will climb directly into orbit with only one intermediate firing by its orbital maneuvering engines. A steeper ascent, made possible by improvements in engine thrust, will save fuel, which may be needed for the rendezvous maneuvers with Solar Max. Once it is 245 miles high, the shuttle will use its remote controlled mechanical arm for another first: The deployment of a 30-foot long cylindrical package, called the long-duration exposure facility (LDEF), which contains 57 separate scientific experiments contributed by nearly 200 scientists in nine countries. LDEF will be left in orbit 10½ months to collect cosmic materials, test solar cells and measure the effects of space on a variety of materials, including 12 million tomato seeds, which will be distributed next year to biology students. Other passengers on the flight: 3,300 honeybees, which are being sent aloft because one collegian wants to see if the insects build the same honeycomb structures in zero-g that they do in normal gravity.

"Now, in a six-day flight that should demonstrate anew the space shuttle's versatility, the orbiter Challenger will attempt to revive Solar Max. If these celestial dramatics succeed, they will represent the space age's first retrieval and repair of an earth satellite.

"The spectacular walk to the satellite should take about 10 minutes. The most breathtaking moment will occur when Nelson threads his way past Solar Max's 7-ft.-long solar panels, which are slicing through space like slow-motion helicopter blades (the satellite rotates once every 6 minutes). If Nelson can dodge this orbital buzz saw without incident, he will try to halt Solar Max's spin.

"In anticipation of just such a rescue, Solar Max's creators equipped the satellite with a pin, or trunnion, near its midriff. It forms a perfect mate with a gadget to be carried by Nelson that looks like a fat bellybutton. NASA calls that protrusion TPAD (for trunnion pin attachment device). Nelson will attach the TPAD to the pin and then fire some of the MMU's thrusters to brake Solar Max's rotation.

"At that point, Challenger will edge to within 30 ft. of the satellite. Then the shuttle's 50-ft.-long, remote-controlled mechanical arm, operated from inside the cockpit by electrical engineer Terry Hart, 37, will lock onto a grappling device on Solar Max . . . (and it) will be eased into a special cradle in the cargo bay for repair. The entire job, from grappling the satellite to installing the new module, should take six hours."

Aviation Week and *Space Technology*, April 16, 1984, give us the answer to the ailing Solar Max Satellite. The headline reads, "Orbiter Crew Restores Solar Max:"

"Retrieval and repair of the Solar Maximum observatory last week fulfilled a space shuttle program goal to develop the capability of servicing satellites in orbit, and in the process demonstrated the ability of the U.S. space program goal to develop the capability of servicing satellites in orbit, and in the process demonstrated the ability of the U.S. space program to recover from a serious setback.

"The Solar Maximum satellite was repaired in the payload bay and returned to orbit April 12."

If the Lord Jesus Christ delays His coming even five years, scientific man will blueprint his grand designs for space stations, space cities and colonies on the moon and possibly even other planets.

Another eye-opening article from *Discover* Magazine is headlined "Welcome to the Cosmic Motel."

"Years and years from now, when people can vacation in a lunar lodge, mine the moons of Jupiter for minerals, and wear silver jumpsuits to work, they will look back on the twentieth century and try to date the beginning of the space age. Some, no doubt, will point to Sputnik, Yuri Gagarin, and John Glenn. Others will recite Neil Armstrong's quote about small and giant steps. But at least a few will cast their votes for the moment when Bruce McCandless levitated out of the space shuttle like a magician's assistant, spinning and rolling as gracefully as a young Rudolf Nureyev. Freed of the tethers that had chained astronauts to their craft in the past, McCandless was at home in space. All he lacked was the house.

"If Ronald Reagan has his way with Congress, such a house will be built by 1992. In his State of the Union speech last January, the President announced that he would order NASA to begin construction of a manned space station — a project that will cost at least $8 billion. 'This nation is at its best when it dares to be great,' he declared. 'We can follow our dreams to distant stars, living and working for peaceful economic scientific gains.'

"The basic design is set: the station must include one living and dining module — called the 'habitat'— one or two interconnected laboratories, a factory, a storage center, and a sort of garage, where the shuttle can dock. Solar panels will provide the power. With these specifications, however, the possible configurations are nearly endless. Now comes the hard job of deciding on one that might work. If all goes well, construction will begin in 1987. Components will be hauled about 250 miles above the earth in a space shuttle's cargo bay, and then pieced together, like a giant Lego set, by the astronauts. The final component should be snapped into place just in time for the 500th anniversary of Columbus' discovery of America, at which point even today's grumpiest scientists and Pentagon officials are likely to find ways to put the station to use. 'My suspicion is that the space station is like the telephone,' says Gerald Griffin, director of the Johnson Space Center. 'No one thought they would need it when it was first invented, but once it was developed, everyone found they couldn't get by without it.' "

Man has traversed his time tunnel with a 360-degree journey and has now returned to Babel. Man is once again bent upon making a name for himself; reaching out farther and farther into outer space, and with God-like fingers to somehow chart his own course among the galaxies of the cosmos.

"And they said, Go to, let us build us a city and a tower, whose top may reach unto heaven; and let us make us a name lest we be scattered abroad upon the face of the whole earth. And the Lord came down to see the city and the tower, which the children of men builded. And the Lord said, Behold, the people is one, and they have all one language; and this they begin to do: and now nothing will be restrained from them, which they have imagined to do" (Genesis 11:4-6).

But God is legally committed to intervene in man's machinations, (Rev. 11:18) and the mighty God of the Bible, the God of time and eternity will come into man's world and will no longer tarry (Hebrews 10:37)!

God will surely bring back those Jews driven into outer space fleeing from the persecution of Antichrist.

"If any of thine be driven out unto the outmost parts of heaven, from thence will the Lord thy God gather thee, and from thence will he fetch thee" (Deuteronomy 30:4).

God also indicates graphically that He will judge the people of the world who continue to rebel against His annointed, the Lord Jesus Christ, during the night-time of this age — the tribulation. And in judgement He will bring back those who flee from the Lord's face into outer space.

"Behold, the days come, saith the Lord God, that I

will send a famine in the land, not a famine of bread, nor a thirst for water, but of hearing the words of the Lord: And they shall wander from sea to sea, and from the north even to the east, they shall run to and fro to seek the word of the Lord, and shall not find it" (Amos 8:11,12).

"I saw the Lord standing upon the altar: and he said, Smite the lintel of the door, that the posts may shake: and cut them in the head, all of them; and I will slay the last of them with the sword: he that fleeth of them shall not flee away, and he that escapeth of them shall not be delivered. Though they dig into hell, thence shall mine hand take them; though they climb up to heaven, thence will I bring them down" (Amos 9:1,2).

At the first coming of Christ there was violence in the heavens; Satan and his kingdom of darkness trying to prevent the first advent of Christ.

We read in Matthew 11:12:

"And from the days of John the Baptist until now the kingdom of heaven suffereth violence, and the violent take it by force."

Many prophetic Scriptures show that the last days will be the time of the violent heavens.

The violence of Satan and his iniquitous traffic are profiled in Ezekiel 28: 14-18:

"Thou art the anointed cherub that covereth; and I have set thee so: thou wast upon the holy mountain of God; thou hast walked up and down in the midst of the stones of fire. Thou wast perfect in thy ways from the day that thou wast created, till iniquity was found in thee. By the multitude of thy merchandise they have filled the midst of thee with violence, and thou hast sinned: therefore I will cast thee as profane out of the mountain of God: and I will destroy thee, O covering cherub, from the midst of the stones of fire. Thine heart was lifted up because of thy beauty, thou hast corrupted thy wisdom by reason of thy brightness: I will cast thee to the ground, I will lay thee before kings, that they may behold thee. Thou hast defiled thy sanctuaries by the multitude of thine iniquities, by the iniquity of thy traffick; therefore will I bring forth a fire from the midst of thee, it shall devour thee, and I will bring thee to ashes upon the earth in the sight of all them that behold thee."

The frenzied activity in space has already begun as man flings out satellites by the thousands and projects space cities and nuclear stations in less than a decade. Already scientists are being selected to experiment on Skylab even without astronaut training.

Quoting *Executive Intelligence Review,* December 13, 1983, page 10, with the headline: "Scientists Join Astronauts on Space Research Frontiers:"

"For the first time in the history of the U.S. Space program, scientists chosen by their peers to do experiments in space have been given the opportunity to work in Earth orbit without having to interrupt their scientific research to be trained as astronauts. For nine days, two scientists are joining a crew of four astronauts to perform more than 70 scientific experiments that cannot be done in the gravity environment of Earth.

"Skylab, a nearly $1 billion facility built by the European Space Agency (ESA) is undergoing its first verification tests in space on the ninth Shuttle mission. The nine-day STS-9 mission, launched on November 28, will relay results to scientists on the ground from experiments in the life sciences, astronomy, solar plasma physics, materials processing, and Earth and atmospheric physics.

"Never before has such a variety of experiments been performed on one flight. Never before have scientists, untrained as astronauts, come straight out of their Earth laboratories to accompany their experiments into space.

"The Space Shuttle provides a launch environment that is so benign that healthy people who are not necessarily in topflight physical condition can make the journey into space. Spacelab provides them with a shirt-sleeve environment where frontier scientific instruments are at their disposal for studying the Earth, the cosmos, and the effects of zero gravity."

In his State of the Union address President Reagan ordered NASA to begin work on a permanently manned space station to be deployed within ten years; big enough to house eight people at the cost of approximately $8 billion.

In the April 23, 1984 *U.S. News And World Report*, James Beggs, head of NASA, and his Russian counterpart discuss "The Race In Space." Among future prospects: manned flight to planets, space stations, star wars antimissile-defense systems in space and possible cooperation between superpowers.

The reappearance of Halley's Comet scheduled for fall of 1985 and the spring of 1986 will surely attract mankind's attention and focus his gaze even more upon the heavens.

Quoting *Astronomy* Magazine, September 1983, an article entitled, "Four Probes To Comet Halley:"

"Comets have long fascinated and terrified the human race. The ancients believed these unpredictable visitors were omens of imminent wars, famines, and pestilence. During the Middle Ages, comets were thought to be fireballs cast down by God as a warning to sinners. Only in the last few centuries have we established their true nature so that scientists regard them not as portends of the future, but Rosetta Stones of the solar systems' remote past. In the 1980s, the people of Earth will, for the first time, send out robot emissaries to greet one of these visitors as it swings by the sun — Comet Halley.

"Halley's comet is by far the most famous. It was the first recognized as being periodic when Edmond Halley predicted its return in 1759. Unfortunately, Halley didn't live to see his prediction fulfilled. When he died in 1742, the fireball-thrown-by-God theory was still in vogue.

"Halley's comet is also fairly bright, as comets go. It orbits the Sun in a great ellipse that brings it to within 88-million kilometers of the Sun at perihelion and out beyond the orbit of Neptune at aphelion. The comet takes about 76 years to complete one orbit and has made at least 29 trips around its course since first being captured. Its first recorded appearance occurred in 240 B.C., its last appearance in 1910, and it will return again in 1986.

"As it turns out, only one bright comet of this type will pass close to Earth in the near future — Comet Halley. All other candidates are either too dim or won't return during this century. Another point in its favor is that a Halley flyby requires one of the lowest launch energies of any comet mission, allowing more sophisticated payloads.

"Several nations are now preparing for the next pass of Halley's comet. Japan, the European Space Agency, the USSR — all are building space probes to be launched in 1984-1985 for a flyby in March 1986. Meanwhile, astronomers everywhere are preparing for extensive ground-based and Earth orbit observations. The International Halley Watch will coordinate these efforts; it has already achieved its first major goal — recovering the comet."

Some eschatology students have thought that Halley's Comet in 1910 might have been a harbinger of the First World War that engulfed the world just four years later. As we consider 1984 and some of the startling predictions for it, we wonder if the only bright comet to visit our solar system in the latter years of this century could be an omen of the coming Antichrist and his system.

The Book of Revelation certainly indicates there will be celestial fire-works during the Tribulation period and especially at the breaking of the sixth seal.

"And I beheld when he had opened the sixth seal, and lo, there was a great earthquake; and the sun became black as sackcloth of hair, and the moon became as blood; And the stars of heaven fell unto the earth, even as a fig tree casteth her untimely figs, when she is shaken of a mighty wind. And the heaven departed as a scroll when it is rolled together, and every mountain and island were moved out of their places" (Revelation 6:12-14).

As more nations acquire the bomb and nuclear capabilities, war in the heavens becomes more of a certainty and a dreaded reality. Russia is obviously preparing for space war.

Consider an article in *Aviation Week* and *Space Technology,* January 2, 1984, entitled "Soviets End Winged Spacecraft Orbital Test Flight In Black Sea."

"The Soviet Union last week launched its third orbital test flight of an unmanned subscale winged shuttle-type spacecraft and recovered it successfully in the Black Sea.

"The launch followed shortly after a congressional report said the Soviets are developing long-range programs for colonies on the Moon and Mars as part of a plan for long-term human habitation in space.

"In a 69-page report on trends in the Soviet space program, it said the Salyut space station program is the 'cornerstone' of an official policy, which looks not only toward a permanent Soviet presence in low-Earth orbit but also toward permanent Soviet settlement of their people on the Moon and Mars. The Soviets take quite seriously the possibility that large numbers of their citizens

will one day live in space. With a sufficient com-
mitment of resources, the Soviets may be able to
maintain a continued human presence in space
through the use of heavy-lift launchers and/or
expanded use of currently available boosters."

It continued: "A shuttle type vehicle would permit routine access to platforms in near-Earth
orbit. A large Salyut complex could serve as a
space transportation node or base camp.

"The office cautioned that Western forecasters
during the past five years had predicted the
Soviets would mount a larger space effort than
they have actually put in place, but added: "The
Soviets have shown considerable perseverance,
and their predictions about even bigger space
stations — capable of housing large collectives
rather than small crews — should be taken seriously."

Two eminent scientists have initiated a petition
urging the United States and the Soviet Union to
ban all weapons from space. The petition is dated
February 24, 1983, one month before President
Reagan's speech advocating a space-based defense against strategic missiles.

I quote from this article "Ban Space Weapons"
as it appeared in the *Bulletin of the Atomic Scientists,* November 1983:

"After American nuclear explosions in space
inadvertently damaged satellites of the United
States and other nations in 1962, most countries
of the world, including the United States and the
Soviet Union, agreed in the Limited Test Ban
Treaty of 1963 never to explode nuclear weapons

in space, in the oceans or in the atmosphere. In 20 years no signatory nation has violated this agreement. Most nations, including the United States and the Soviet Union, also adhere to the Outer Space Treaty of 1967 banning from space all weapons of mass destruction, and, specifically, all nuclear weapons. But fiction writers and military strategists have for about a century romanticized the purported inevitability of warfare in space. The use of non-nuclear weapons of more limited lethality than 'mass destruction,' while forbidden on other celestial bodies by the 1967 treaty, is still permitted in Earth orbit, and in cislunar, circumplanetary and interplanetary space.

"We believe that the testing or deployment of any weapons in space — in part by threatening vital satellite assets — significantly increases the likelihood of warfare on Earth."

An exotic and sensitive technology is shaping up as a sleeping issue with explosive potential in the 1984 U.S. elections. Specifically, the issue is reconnaisance satellite technology and capability.

A good deal of hyperbole, of public relations banners, has surrounded reconnaissance satellite imagery in the past. Claims that license plate numbers on a parked car could be read from orbital altitudes served an obvious political purpose in the era of Henry Kissinger, Jimmy Carter and the pursuit of detente. If the all-seeing eye in space could detect anything anywhere on the ground, or so the public was led to believe, it followed that an arms control agreement was safely verifiable.

In all the talk of shuttles, space stations and spies in the skies, it becomes evident that whoever controls outer space will be the dominant nation in the world.

Aviation Week & Space Technology, January 16, 1984, headlines the ambitious plans the United States has for space exploration: "National Aeronautics and Space Administration plans to launch 12 expendable vehicles in 1984 in addition to 10 manned space shuttle missions."

The next week, *Aviation Week & Space Technology,* January 23, 1984 gives further details under the heading, "NASA Budget Includes Station Funding:"

"The definition of an $8 billion U.S. space station project will be accelerated by addition of $150-$175 million to the National Aeronautics and Space Administration's new budget and an expected call by President Reagan this week for a permanent U.S. presence in space that later could expand beyond a station to such objectives as U.S. colonization of the Moon and manned flights to Mars.

"Under this approach a U.S. station facility could be operational by 1992. The Johnson Space Center will lead the development with substantial participation by the Marshall and Goddard space flight centers."

Here's a scientific project right out of *Star Wars*: "The Manned Space Cruiser":

"Space cruiser manned research vehicle under study by the Defense Advanced Research Projects Agency and SCS Corp., Alexanderia, VA, would perform the same flight test role for new systems and concepts in space as those undertaken for atmospheric flight by the X-aircraft series begun more than 35 years ago with the Bell X-1. The space cruiser concept would be a 26.5-foot long 10,000-pound vehicle with small payload bays located in the foldable nose and between the aft engine nozzles. The pilot would fly in an unpressurized open cockpit environment wearing a space suit. A dome over the pilot in this version provides micrometeorite protection. The space cruiser could be launched by the space shuttle, fired into space on top of an MX missile or air-launched from a Boeing 747.

"An addition of external propellant tanks or a propulsion module such as the General Dynamics wide-body Centaur could result in flight capabilities to geosynchronous orbit, the Moon, or the ability to maneuver extensively large, externally mounted payloads in Earth orbit.

"The space cruiser also would be capable of high-velocity descents into the atmosphere where the vehicle then could either fly back up into space or make a parafoil landing to complete its mission."

We can safely conclude that the nations of the world are preparing to inhabit the heavenlies, to push back the frontiers of space and to reach out with God-like fingers. We have every reason to believe that God will again intervene in the kingdoms of men and this time He is going to set the world straight. In other words, He will put the earth back on its axis as it was before the flood.

Science, March 1984 edition, has an interesting item that could have a Bible correlation. It is entitled "Is The Earth's Field Heading For A Flip?"

"The Earth's magnetic field has decreased in strength more than 50 percent the last 4,000 years. So says geophysicists Subir Banerjee and Donald Sprowl, who suggest the decrease could indicate the beginning of a reversal of the Earth's magnetic poles. After a reversal, compasses will point south instead of north."

The only space ship I am really interested in is God's Fiery Chariot (Isaiah 66:15) manned by angelic beings who will catch away every blood-bought born-again believer to prepared heavenly places (John 14:1-3) before He rises to shake both heaven and earth in preparation for the coming kingdom of our great God and Saviour Jesus Christ (Hebrews 12:26-29).

8

FACING THE FUTURE

If the 1980s were apocalyptic, the uncharted 1990s — as a space bridge or time tunnel — will hurl the human masses precipitously into the 21st Century.

According to *Modern Maturity*, February-March 1984:

"Life in the 21st Century. What lies ahead? Who can tell? The future is not engraved in stone and we do not walk a foreordained path. We make our own future and we can be as foolish or as wise as we choose. If our choice is to explode in a thermo-nuclear war, or to go down the tube into a creeping sludge of pollution, then there will be no future worth describing. But what if we are wise and make the most of advancing technology, using it humanely and prudently? In that case the future may be bright indeed. For instance: The two enormous technological advances in the coming decades, advances that we are certain of, because they are already here, are 1. computerization, and 2. expansion into space. Both are gifts of the human mind and spirit that will be difficult to control but, if well-controlled, will lead us far. Computerization already has taken over modern societies in an irreversible manner. That is, we cannot abandon all our computers in a society like that of the United States in 1984 without government, industry and the military all breaking down. Since the alternative is chaos, we can only move ahead. And we are moving ahead."

Author Isaac Asimov believes that home computers are going to become as much a part of the American family over the next quarter-century as television did in the 25 years after 1950.

"You can employ them as a word-processor; an information-gathering device. News of the day, up-to-date stock-market reports, weather reports, bank data, shopping data, are all examples of their extensive use. They may be used to place orders with one's broker, travel agent, banker, or at the shopping mall. Laser light will substitute for microwaves, so that there will be millions of TV channels available so every individual might have one entirely his own. The computer can be hooked up to the contents of a huge computerized library."

Futurist authors such as Isaac Asimov and Carl Sagan blithely speak of the future in glowing terms of the New Age. But if it were not for the providence and intervention of Almighty God, the dark side of the future and the force (Satan) would render planet earth as barren and dark as the moon.

WorldView '84 is a congress of approximately 500 leading thinkers from around the world who met in Washington D.C. June 10 -14, 1984. One report said:

"The theme of WorldView '84 was carefully chosen to emphasize that the world is now in a critical period where important choices must be made concerning the human future. Stupendous advances are occurring in communications, electronics, biotechnology, and space exploration. At the same time there are mounting and potentially explosive problems.

"The committee planning WorldView '84 has decided that the emphasis at the conference should be placed on identifying possible solutions to significant problems rather than merely discussing the nature and extent of the problems. During this time of soul-searching amid faltering economic systems and international tensions, it is important to remember that there are many potential solutions to world problems."

One headline read: "Congress Takes Active Interest In WorldView '84."

"Participation in the Fifth General Assembly is expected to surpass that of the 1982 General Assembly, when 12 members of Congress participated. Already confirmed for positions on the program are Senators Spark Matsunaga and Claiborne Pell and Representatives Bob Edgar, Berkley Bedell, and Claudine Schneider. Many others have tentatively committed to participate and will confirm these commitments as the congressional schedule becomes more clear."

Some of the topics for discussion at this world congress are: the evolution and impacts of robotics; future prospects for sustained global peace; and world order models project views of the future world order.

This world congress is sponsored by the World Future Society headquartered in Bethesda, Maryland. It would appear that the futurists are getting their program in high gear and will march forth with man-made solutions to solve all the world's ills.

One of the pressing problems the Globalists hope to solve by the year 2000 is the exploding mass of population.

Tad Szulc writes somberly in his article, "One Person Too Many?" carried in *Parade* Magazine, April 29, 1984:

"Short of nuclear annihilation, the greatest threat to humanity is, ironically, its own sheer mass. Global population grows inexorably and at a rate so prodigious that by the year 2000 — only 16 years from now — the world, with its added billions, will be unable to provide adequate food and energy, let alone jobs, housing, education and health care. And what could happen by the mid-21st century (when babies born in this decade approach old age) defies imagination — unless acceptable ways are found of curtailing population growth. This is as true in a special way for the United States as it is generally for the developing Third World, which accounts for 75 percent of the world's population.

"Overpopulation on the scale currently taking shape will result in new and greater famines, perhaps wars, civil strife and deep social distortions as well as massive malnutrition and disease, vast migration and a sharp drop in living standards almost everywhere, including this country. Yet no high-priority international strategy exists to cope with these problems. Emergency assistance is essentially all that is being done by the world community.

"Demographers have long warned that massive overpopulation is a time bomb, but in 1983 the point was finally reached when the threat began to become a reality. Recent discussions with population specialists at the UN, World Bank, U.S. Bureau of the Census and Washington think-tanks reveal this gloomy picture: The World population rose by 82 million between mid-1982 and mid-1983 — an all time record, making 1983 a demographic turning point — reaching 4.7 billion last September. This is more than twice the global population of 20 years ago. The Census Bureau projects an increase of 82.8 million in 1983/84 and 84 million by 1986 and 6.2 billion by 2000."

The great flood came in the days when men began to multiply on the face of the earth (Genesis 6:1). Evidently a similar cataclysm is rapidly building up and no one seems to have the answer.

Jesus warns "But as the days of Noah were, so shall also the coming of the Son of Man be" (Matthew 24:37).

Continuing to quote from the article "One Person Too Many?" :

"The UN has a population devision with a relatively low priority. The World Bank's efforts are confined to studies and recommendations. The UN Food and Agriculture Organization lacks adequate resources. The Reagan Administration has a Coordinator of Population Affairs — a scarcely visible operation — in the State Department. Also buried in the State Department is a small Directorate for Health and Population in the Agency for International Development.

"Meanwhile, the population time bomb is ticking. When the explosion comes at the end of this century the United States will not escape the fallout unless we assume leadership to help our species save itself from its own blindness."

This propaganda to prepare the people for the Globalist 2000 program which proposes to reduce the population of planet earth to two billion by the year 2000 by implementing and encouraging euthanasia, abortion, suicide and homosexuality.

Scientists are well aware that we are living in a different world to that of 50 years ago and that the atomic cloud is hovering like a black harbinger of doom over every nation.

On the cover of the *Bulletin Of The Atomic Scientists* appears these apocalyptic words:

"This is a time when things must be done before their time" (Robert Redfield).

On page three of the same *Bulletin* there is a somber warning about nuclear fratricide entitled "Perspectives for 1984."

"Not since the frightening days of the Cuban missile crisis has the world seemed so perilously close to World War III.

"If it is possible to stand back and to view the international situation with any degree of detachment, what one sees is very frightening indeed. It is not only a question of the number of nuclear weapons poised in hair trigger readiness for launching by both sides — although this number is now in the tens of thousands, from small battlefield firecrackers to multi-megaton city busters deployed in a variety of vehicles, from artillery shells to intercontinental ballistic missiles. More ominous is the inclination of the leaders of the nuclear powers to talk and act as though they were prepared to use these weapons under a variety of circumstances which are all too plausible."

The Bible explicitly describes nuclear judgments that will come upon the world during the tribulation time period.

"And this shall be the plague wherewith the Lord will smite all the people that have fought against Jerusalem; Their flesh shall consume away while they stand upon their feet, and their eyes shall consume away in their holes and their tongue shall consume away in their mouth. And it shall come to pass in that day, that a great tumult from the Lord shall be among them; and they shall lay hold every one on the hand of his neighbor, and his hand shall rise up against the hand of his neighbor" (Zechariah 14:12, 13).

According to the "White Paper" by John Wesley White, issues 27 and 28:

"In a major plenary session Dr. Bernard Lown, president of the INTERNATIONAL PHYSICIANS

FOR THE PREVENTION OF NUCLEAR WAR warned ominously: 'We are doomed. People must coerce their governments to stop this race to Armageddon' (Toronto Star, June 8, 1983) (this exhortation doesn't work well in the Soviet Union, where the news leaked out that yet another Russian who tried to 'urge' — not 'coerce' his 'government' to 'stop this race to Armageddon' was imprisoned unconditionally in June, and without a trial for — perhaps a lifetime).

"Dr. Down, professor of cardiology at Harvard noted that a U.S. Senate committee reported there were 3,703 false alarms in the early warning system in an 18-month-period— with 147 of them serious enough to require evaluation ... four that 'nearly led to a nuclear exchange.' Human fallibility can play an even more important role ... 115,000 U.S. military personnel have 'critical access' to nuclear weapons or their control. The problems seem, for man, insurmountable! A great deal of controversy has been attached to THE NATIONAL FILM BOARD OF CANADA'S anti-nuclear short: 'If you Love This Planet,' which won an Oscar in April. The Russians loved it's attack on U.S. nuclear policy (UPI April 15, 1984). It's message is terribly solemn. In it Dr. Helen Haldicut in warning of impending 'nuclear catastrophe' calculates there's a 50/50 chance of nuclear war in the mid 1980's.

"Amos ... warns that impenitent man destines himself for war. Jesus warned that unprecedented war would precede His coming. Revelation 9:15 omens the 'day and hour, and now (they) kill a third of all mankind.' Let's quote the Soviets! Dr. Frank

Sommers, a Toronto psychiatrist and chairman of Physicians for Social Responsibility reports during a current trip to Russia: 'A Soviet survey predicted a third of all humanity would be killed in a nuclear exchange' (same figure as Albert Einstein and the aged Apostle John projected) (Tor. Star June 28, 1983). But what would it take to trigger such a catastrophe? The World Assembly for Peace and Life and Against Nuclear War met in Prague and voiced the thinking of 2,500 delegates from 132 countries:

"Humanity stands at a crucial cross roads of history. One step in the wrong direction — and the world could be irrevocably thrown into the abyss of nuclear war.

"Mere statistics indicate that the atomic stockpiles of the nuclear nations of the world are more than enough to reduce this planet to a lifeless state. By 1985, 35 nations will have atomic or hydrogen bombs. It is all too evident that the nations of the world are preparing for Armageddon."

"The first angel sounded, and there followed hail and fire mingled with blood, and they were cast upon the earth: and the third part of trees was burnt up, and all green grass was burnt up. And the second angel sounded, and as it were a great mountain burning with fire was cast into the sea: and the third part of the sea became blood; And the third part of the creatures which were in the sea, and had life, died; and the third part of the ships were destroyed. And the third angel sounded, and there fell a great star from heaven, burning as it were a lamp, and it fell upon the third part of the rivers, and upon the fountains of waters; And the name of the star is called Wormwood: and the third part of the waters became wormwood; and many men died of the waters, because they were made bitter. And the fourth angel sounded, and the third part of the sun was smitten, and the third part of the moon, and the third part of the stars; so as the third part of them was darkened, and the day shone not for a third part of it, and the night likewise" (Revelation 8:7-12).

These verses just quoted describe what will happen when the nuclear holocaust comes. There will be no place to hide, although men will seek shelter in that day (See Revelation 6:15, 16). The only hiding place is in Christ Jesus: the way, the truth and the life (John 14:6). All the events in this chapter indicate that a nuclear confrontation could happen before the end of this decade!

In looking to the future, man desperately seeks peace. But all the evidence indicates that peace will continue to elude man as the stockpiling of nuclear weapons escalate and the nations of the world prepare for space war, computer war and nuclear holocaust.

A publication called *Peace For Israel 1984* addresses this subject very succinctly on the inside cover under the heading "Seeking Peace in a Troubled World."

"Mankind is on the threshold of some of the greatest climactic events in history! Will the world soon be facing Armageddon, or will there be a time of peace and prosperity such as the world has never seen? Recent headlines and statements of outstanding news sources and world leaders indicate a grave concern exists concerning where mankind is headed:

★ "Is the whole world going broke?" *Chicago Tribune*

★ "Bankers Meet in Toronto, See Possible World Chaos." *Star News Service*

★ "Fahd Enjoins the Arabs to Launch Holy War Against Israel." *Miami Herald*

★ "Global Terrorism About to Explode." *The McAlvany Intelligence Advisor*

"Yet there are some who believe the world is getting better. *U.S. News And World Report,* July 11, 1983 stated:

"'At a time when much of the world seems to be at peace, no fewer than a fourth of the nations around the globe are caught up in armed conflict. More than forty countries are involved in hostilities of one form or another that have claimed as many as five million lives.' "

Is the world really at peace? With respect to "peace and prosperity" an interesting statement is found in the Scriptures:

"For when they shall say peace and safety then sudden destruction cometh upon them ..."

Many who would like to know what the future holds, are asking questions such as: "Will America survive? Will communism be the winner? Is a world leader about to emerge who will lead the entire world? Will a world government soon arise? Are computers going to be used to control people? Will humans be branded with a 'mark'? Can Israel survive when all the nations come against her? Where will it all end?"

Are computers going to be used to control people?

The answer is an unequivocal yes.

Computers are already — to some extent — controlling banking and business. Much of commerce and travel are also controlled or regulated by computers. As we read about smart robots, Fifth Generation computers that are compatible with man's brain, microchips and biotechnology, it seems inevitable that a computerized technological system like "Big Brother" will one day — perhaps in the near future — control the nations of the world.

An article from *Systems*, written by Robert J. Clermen who is with the Mitre Corporation, U.S.A., should cause every Bible student to immediately begin to think about the image of the beast that has life (Rev. 13:15).

The article is entitled *Combining Biology And Electronics*:

"Two fields of technology, microelectronics and biotechnology, are prime candidates to dominate industrial innovation over the remainder of this century. After more than 20 years of rapid growth, semi-conductor technology is now incorporated in common household appliances as well as the most advanced electronics, such as high-speed computers and industrial robots. Biotechnology, by harnessing the power of the gene through recombinant DNA techniques, is likely to have an equally significant impact on industry and the quality of life. Biotechnology is younger (just over ten years old), and the first commercial products are now entering the marketplace."

Please take note that terms like genes, DNA and biotechnology indicate living matter; and they are essential parts of a human entity made in the likeness of God.

Again quoting from *Systems*:

"At a molecular scale, biological systems have many characteristics that are desirable in micro-electronic components, including small size, complex function, nondissipative conduction, and low power requirements. At the scale of cells and organisms, living systems exhibit desirable features such as parallel processing, pattern recognition, and intelligence. The goal of those involved in bioelectronics research is to exploit these desirable properties of biological systems in order to produce electronic logic and memory devices that will exceed today's very large-scale integrated circuit (VLSI) technology by as much as nine orders of magnitude in size and performance."

This futurist article involves the cooperation of biologists and electrical engineers as well as chemists, physicists, and computer scientists.

The four groupings of these researchers are:

★ Molecular biologists working on the biological building blocks for device fabrication.

★ Theoretical chemists seeking to synthesize chemical analogues for the circuits and switches of conventional devices.

★Computer and information scientists developing new device architectures that mimic biological information processing.

★Physicists and electrical engineers working on problems of signal processing and input/output at a molecular scale.

We continue to quote from *Systems* under the heading "A New Approach to Computation."

"It is interesting to note that much of the above research is aimed at producing binary switches. The presumption is that bioelectronic devices will be used to do digital computations. There is a group of computer and information scientists who are questioning this presumption and suggesting that new computer architectures that are not composed solely of binary switches will be required to fully exploit the potential of bioelectronics. One model for study is information processing in the nervous systems of higher organisms. The idea that neurons act as switching elements, analogous to the switching elements of a computer, was popularized in the 1950s with the demonstration that networks of neurons could implement the computing functions of a digital computer. This concept is being re-evaluated based on recent research suggesting that information processing in the brain, for example, may be a function of molecular scale processes within the neuron, as well as the relatively macroscale processes of neuron firing. As this group advances our understanding of biological information processing, including the processes that lead to pattern recognition and intelligence, their findings should help to guide bioelectronics in the development of radically different approaches to computation."

In the final quotation, the cooperating scientists talk about the nervous system, the human brain and radically different approaches to computation. It does not require stretching the imagination to consider lifelike robots performing routine tasks, humanoids or even the image of the beast that has life.

"And he had power to give life unto the image of the beast, that the image of the beast should both speak, and cause that as many as would not worship the image of the beast should be killed. And he causeth all, both small and great, rich and poor, free and bond, to receive a mark in their right hand, or in their foreheads" (Revelation 13:15, 16).

For more than a decade we have suggested that the image of the beast that has life, and will be able to speak and control all the people of the world, could be a giant robot empowered by sophisticated electronic circuitry and/or electronic chips.

Here's a description of the ultimate computer from a secular publication, *National Enquirer*, December 13, 1983, in an article entitled *"A Super Computer Will Solve All Our Problems — And Even Crack Jokes."*

"The ultimate computer will look like a giant robot and act like a human being — making lightning-fast decisions on its own, feeling human emotions like friendship, and even cracking jokes.

"There will be one super-brain for the whole world. Housed in a 10-foot-high body, it will search out and solve mankind's problems — crime, ill health, bad weather, traffic jams, etc.

"That's how futurists like Saul Kent — author of *The Life-Extension Revolution* — visualize the ultimate computer of tomorrow.

" 'The ultimate computer will not only be endowed with many human characteristics, designers will construct it in a human-like form so they can treat it as much like a human as possible,' said Kent.

" 'It could be a colossal robot up to 10 feet high — and it will be mobile, able to move itself in case of a war. And it will develop traits characteristic of a human personality.' "

You can readily see that this giant lifelike robot would be very impressive, and of course, in the beginning it would be helping people, so this electronic superhero would be the good guy in this end-time scenario. But a colossus with these electronic capabilities could easily become the "Big Brother" watching you or the Beast system (see Rev. 13).

Today there is an international race to determine which nation will dominate the computer market.

Quoting from the magazine *Proceedings Of The Institute Of Electrical And Electronics Engineers*, January 1984 in an article entitled "Science, Industry, and the New Japanese Challenge":

"The Japanese Super-Speed Computer project has as its goal the design of computers for scientific applications which would be about one hundred times more powerful than today's most powerful supercomputers ... the CRAY-1 and CRAY X-MP from Cray Research Inc., the Control Data Corporation CDG 205, the Denelcor HEP... and ... the Floating Point Systems FPS-164 ... The Japanese supercomputers could handle far more of the existing U.S. scientific and engineering computing load than any U.S. supercomputer... The Japanese Super-Speed Computer project... aimed at designing a supercomputer one hundred times more powerful than existing systems by 1990. It is this project which is setting the time scale for U.S. action. In particular it means the Japanese are seeking a major improvement in supercomputer performance."

"The Fifth Generation computer project aims at incorporating artificial intelligence into computing systems with logical inference capability used for natural-language interpretations and the like. These new smart moves will be ready in the immediate future at just the time the market demands will explode. American and European competitors are now gearing up to meet this exciting new challenge.

"Do you realize what this all means? Within the next six years Fifth Generation computers will supersede our current most sophisticated supercomputers. Engineers have developed a robot that has a TV camera's eyes, temperature — and radiation-measuring sensors, and multijointed arms capable of complicated operations. Now we have robots which speak, obey spoken commands, identify shapes of objects, but they are mere prototypes of smart robots. Robots are just one application, and robots are already making other robots! In less than six years supercomputers will be one hundred times more powerful."

Popular Science, June 1984 reported:

"TV firms are readying receivers with computer chips that replace hundreds of components and process video in digital form. Computerized picture and sound circuits simplify TV alignment, noise and ghost reduction, teletext and videotex reception, and compensation for component aging. They also make possible many totally new features, such as freeze frame, color pictures within a picture, zoom, 1,000-line images, automatic VCR programming, and more.

"Last fall, at the world's largest consumer electronics show in West Berlin, a Panasonic engineer gave me what looked like an ordinary TV infrared remote control. But when I used it, I learned that the matching 19-inch color receiver that I flicked commands at was far from ordinary.

"The set, in a show demonstration room, had all the features of a current high-end model. Glowing in one corner of the main TV picture, though, was a separate five-inch TV image. One of the remote's many functions enabled me to instantly reverse these independent pictures: When I tapped a button, the small picture filled the screen, and the big image collapsed into a corner. But unlike earlier picture-within-a picture sets I'd seen, with monochrome, coarse, grainy auxiliary images, this prototype model displayed two full-resolution color pictures.

"Panasonic's receiver and other TV models at the show were the first glimpse given to the public of the most revolutionary change in television sets at least since the introduction of color — possibly of all time. These were digital TV sets — in effect, sophisticated computers that act as television receivers."

Please notice that your television receiver becomes a complicated computer with an image. Also notice the statement, "glowing in one corner of the main TV image." Thus, the image of the beast could be projected in the corner of your television screen during regular programming and at all times.

As we observe the developing technology and the tentacles of bureaucratic control moving ever closer, the image of the beast or "Big Brother" comes into sharper focus. The picture for planet Earth is a dark one. The demon forces of Satan are converging on the four corners of the earth.

The prince of prophecy (Rev. 19:10) bids us watch for that shining light of prophetic revelation as it shines into our hearts.

"We have also a more sure word of prophecy; whereunto ye do well that ye take heed, as unto a light that shineth in a dark place, until the day dawn, and the day star arise in your hearts: Knowing this first, that no prophecy of the scripture is of any private interpretation. For the prophecy came not in old time by the will of man: but holy men of God spake as they were moved by the Holy Ghost" (II Peter 1:19-21).

MORE FAITH-BUILDING BOOKS
BY HUNTINGTON HOUSE

GLOBALISM: AMERICA'S DEMISE, By William Bowen, Jr., $8.95 (hard back). The Globalists — some of the most powerful people on earth — have plans to totally eliminate God, the family and the United States as we know it today.

Globalism is the vehicle the humanists are using to implement their secular humanistic philosophy to bring about their one-world government.

This book clearly alerts Christians to what the Globalists have planned for them.

MURDERED HEIRESS . . . LIVING WITNESS, by Dr. Petti Wagner, $5.95. This is the book of the year about Dr. Petti Wagner — heiress to a large fortune — who was kidnapped and murdered for her wealth, yet through a miracle of God lives today.

Dr. Wagner did indeed endure a horrible death experience, but through God's mercy, she had her life given back to her to serve Jesus and help suffering humanity.

Some of the events recorded in the book are terrifying. But the purpose is not to detail a violent murder conspiracy but to magnify the glorious intervention of God.

THE HIDDEN DANGERS OF THE RAINBOW: The New Age Movement and Our Coming Age of Barbarism, by Constance Cumbey, $5.95. A national best-seller, this book exposes the New Age Movement which is made up of tens of thousands of organizations throughout the world. The movement's goal is to set up a one-world order under the leadership of a false christ.

Mrs. Cumbey is a trial lawyer from Detroit, Mich., and has spent years exposing the New Age Movement and the false christ.

TRAINING FOR TRIUMPH: A Handbook for Mothers and Fathers, by Dr. W. George Selig and Deborah D. Cole, $4.95. Being a good mother and father is one of life's great challenges. However, most parents undertake that challenge with little or no preparation, according to Dr. Selig, a professor at CBN University. He says that often, after a child's early years are past, parents sigh: "Where did we go wrong?"

Dr. Selig, who has 20 years of experience in the field of education, carefully explains how to be good mothers and fathers and how to apply good principles and teachings while children are still young.

Feel Better and Live Longer Through: THE DIVINE CONNECTION, by Dr. Donald Whitaker $4.95. This is a Christian's guide to life extension. Dr. Whitaker of Longview, Texas, says you really can feel better and live longer by following Biblical principles set forth in the Word of God.

THE DIVINE CONNECTION shows you how to experience divine health, a happier life, relief from stress, a better appearance, a healthier outlook, a zest for living and a sound emotional life. And much, much more.

THE AGONY OF DECEPTION by Ron Rigsbee

with Dorothy Bakker, $6.95. Ron Rigsbee was a man who through surgery became a woman and now through the grace of God is a man again. This book — written very tastefully — is the story of God's wonderful grace and His miraculous deliverance of a disoriented young man. It offers hope for millions of others trapped in the agony of deception.

THE DAY THEY PADLOCKED THE CHURCH, by E. Edward Roe, $3.50. The warm yet heartbreaking story of Pastor Everett Sileven, a Nebraska Baptist pastor, who was jailed and his church padlocked because he refused to bow to Caesar. It is also the story of 1,000 Christians who stood with Pastor Sileven, in defying Nebraska tyranny in America's crisis of freedom.

BACKWARD MASKING UNMASKED — Backward Satanic Messages of Rock and Roll Exposed, By Jacob Aranz, $4.95.

Are rock and roll stars using the technique of backward masking to implant their own religious and moral values into the minds of young people? Are these messages satanic, drug-related and filled with sexual immorality? Jacob Aranza answers these and other questions.

SCOPES II/THE GREAT DEBATE, by Louisiana State Senator Bill Keith, 193 pages, $4.95.

Senator Keith's book strikes a mortal blow at evolution which is the cornerstone of the religion of secular humanism. He explains what parents and others can do to assure that creation science receives equal time in the school classrooms, where Christian children's faith is being destroyed.

WHY J. R.? A Psychiatrist Discusses the Villain of Dallas, by Dr. Lew Ryder, 152 pages, $4.95.

An eminent psychiatrist explains how the anti-Christian religion of Secular Humanism has taken over television programming and what Christians can do to fight back.

NEED A MIRACLE? by Harald Bredesen, 159 pages, $4.95.

This book shows how to draw upon the greatest power in the universe to cope with "unsolvable" problems; "incurable" illnesses; enslaving habits; and day-to-day money shortages.

YES, LORD! by Harald Bredesen, 198 pages, $4.95.

This is a wonderful story of God's power and grace. Pat Boone said: "Knowing Harald Bredesen is a little like knowing Elijah. Miracles follow him wherever he goes."

YES, send me the following books:

_____ copy (copies) of **God's Timetable For The 1980's** @ $5.95 = _____

_____ copy (copies) of **Globalism: America's Demise** @ $8.95 = _____

_____ copy (copies) of **Murdered Heiress . . . Living Witness** @ $5.95 = _____

_____ copy (copies) of **The Hidden Dangers of the Rainbow** @ $5.95 = _____

_____ copy (copies) of **The Divine Connection** @ $4.95 = _____

_____ copy (copies) of **The Agony of Deception** @ $6.95 = _____

_____ copy (copies) of **Training for Triumph** @ $4.95 = _____

_____ copy (copies) of **The Day They Padlocked The Church** @ $3.50 = _____

_____ copy (copies) of **Backward Masking Unmasked** @ $4.95 = _____

_____ copy (copies) of **Scopes II/The Great Debate** @ $4.95 = _____

_____ copy (copies) of **Why J.R.?** @ $4.95 = _____

_____ copy (copies) of **Need A Miracle?** @ $4.95 = _____

_____ copy (copies) of **Yes, Lord!** @ $4.95 = _____

Enclosed is: $ _____ including postage (please include $1 per book for postage) for

_____ books.

Name _____

Address _____

City and State _____ Zip _____

Mail to Huntington House, Inc., P. O. Box 78205, Shreveport, Louisiana 71137

Telephone Orders: (TOLL FREE) 1-800-572-8213, or in Louisiana (318) 237-7049